T0334646

Cambridge Elements ≡

Elements in Applied Evolutionary Science
edited by
David F. Bjorklund
Florida Atlantic University

THE HIDDEN TALENTS FRAMEWORK

Implications for Science, Policy, and Practice

Bruce J. Ellis
University of Utah

Laura S. Abrams
University of California, Los Angeles

Ann S. Masten
University of Minnesota, Twin Cities

Robert J. Sternberg
Cornell University

Nim Tottenham
Columbia University

Willem E. Frankenhuis
Utrecht University and Max Planck Institute for Research on Crime, Security and Law

CAMBRIDGE
UNIVERSITY PRESS

CAMBRIDGE
UNIVERSITY PRESS

Shaftesbury Road, Cambridge CB2 8EA, United Kingdom

One Liberty Plaza, 20th Floor, New York, NY 10006, USA

477 Williamstown Road, Port Melbourne, VIC 3207, Australia

314–321, 3rd Floor, Plot 3, Splendor Forum, Jasola District Centre,
New Delhi – 110025, India

103 Penang Road, #05–06/07, Visioncrest Commercial, Singapore 238467

Cambridge University Press is part of Cambridge University Press & Assessment,
a department of the University of Cambridge.

We share the University's mission to contribute to society through the pursuit of
education, learning and research at the highest international levels of excellence.

www.cambridge.org
Information on this title: www.cambridge.org/9781009350068

DOI: 10.1017/9781009350051

First published 2023

A catalogue record for this publication is available from the British Library.

ISBN 978-1-009-35006-8 Paperback
ISSN 2752-9428 (online)
ISSN 2752-941X (print)

The Hidden Talents Framework

Implications for Science, Policy, and Practice

Elements in Applied Evolutionary Science

DOI: 10.1017/9781009350051

First published online: March 2023

Bruce J. Ellis
University of Utah

Laura S. Abrams
University of California, Los Angeles

Ann S. Masten
University of Minnesota, Twin Cities

Robert J. Sternberg
Cornell University

Nim Tottenham
Columbia University

Willem E. Frankenhuis
Utrecht University and Max Planck Institute for Research on Crime, Security and Law

Author for correspondence: Bruce J. Ellis, bruce.ellis@psych.utah.edu

Abstract: Although early-life adversity can undermine healthy development, an evolutionary-developmental perspective implies that children growing up in harsh environments will develop intact, or even *enhanced*, skills for solving problems in high-adversity contexts (i.e., "hidden talents"). This Element situates the hidden talents model within a larger interdisciplinary framework. Summarizing theory and research on hidden talents, it proposes that stress-adapted skills represent a form of adaptive intelligence enabling individuals to function within the constraints of harsh environments. It discusses potential applications of this perspective to multiple sectors concerned with youth from harsh environments, including education, social services, and juvenile justice, and compares the hidden talents model with contemporary developmental resilience models. The hidden talents approach, it concludes, offers exciting directions for research on childhood adversity, with translational implications for leveraging stress-adapted skills to more effectively tailor education, jobs, and interventions to fit the needs of individuals from a diverse range of life circumstances.

Keywords: adaptive intelligence, early adversity, educational interventions, resilience, developmental adaptation to stress

ISBNs: 9781009350068 (PB), 9781009350051 (OC)

ISSNs: 2752-9428 (online), 2752-941X (print)

Contents

1 Introduction

One out of four adults in the United States reports having had at least three adverse childhood experiences (e.g., child abuse or neglect, incarceration of a family member, family dissolution), with the highest rates of adversity among people in the lowest income and education brackets (Merrick et al., 2018). Decades of research has shown that people who experience such childhood adversities, and particularly those who grow up in poverty, tend to score lower on standard cognitive tests and tasks, such as traditional measures of IQ, language, and executive functioning (e.g., Duncan et al., 2017; Ursache & Noble, 2016). These findings have reinforced the persistence of *deficit models* in research on young people exposed to adversity, suggesting that chronic stress impairs brain structure and function in ways that undermine social and cognitive abilities.

Deficit perspectives are central in prominent theories of stress and development such as cumulative risk (e.g., Evans et al., 2013; Felitti et al., 1998), diathesis stress (e.g., Monroe & Simons, 1991), allostatic load (Lupien et al. 2006; McEwen & Stellar 1993), and the dimensional model of adversity (e.g., McLaughlin et al., 2014). Theory and research in this domain has focused on the harmful effects of early adversity – a focus that has guided social policy and practice toward *mitigating risk* (e.g., poverty reduction, improving the quality of parent-child relationships in stressful contexts, providing safe places for children such as Boys & Girls Clubs) and/or *ameliorating deficits* (e.g., fostering executive function skills, improving literacy and numeracy skills, enhancing social and emotional learning). These intervention strategies are important and, in some cases, have achieved meaningful success in improving the circumstances and outcomes of adversity-exposed children and families (e.g., Blair & Raver, 2014; Deming, 2009; Durlack et al., 2011; Reynolds et al., 2019).

Despite this achievement, intervention strategies focused on mitigating risk and ameliorating deficits – however well-intentioned – are imbalanced with respect to recognizing strengths as well as weaknesses that may arise in contexts of adversity. Consequently, we know much more about the vulnerabilities of adversity-exposed people than we know about their strengths. This imbalance affects how the general public, policy makers, educators, and others view people with a history of adversity, including how adversity-exposed people see themselves. Such perceptions can be disrespectful as well as distressing to members of marginalized and low-income communities with a history of adverse experiences. As one community stakeholder noted, "there is a tendency to look at people from underserved communities as somehow inferior" (Acosta et al., 2016, p. 40). More generally, the focus on adversity-related risks and deficits reinforces negative stereotypes and biases against adversity-exposed people (see Barbarin et al., 2020). For instance, the much-publicized "30-million-word gap" (Hart & Risley, 1995) – the idea that children from low-income families hear far fewer words than their affluent counterparts – leads teachers not only to perceive students from economically marginalized and minoritized backgrounds as lacking in school readiness, but to narrow their learning experiences accordingly (Adair et al., 2017). Likewise, widely reported research on the deleterious effects of early adversity on brain development may bias teachers' perceptions of the capacities and potential of stress-exposed students, already viewing them as lacking in skills and knowledge that are needed for success when they enter school, and thus promoting a remedial rather than a growth-based mindset and pedagogy.

In addition to the potential harm caused to children and communities, deficit-based approaches are limited by an error of omission: they critically miss the social and cognitive skills that develop *in response to adversity* (Ellis et al., 2017; Ellis, Abrams et al., 2022; Frankenhuis & de Weerth, 2013; Frankenhuis, Young, et al., 2020). We refer to these skills as *hidden talents* – hidden because they have been largely invisible to scientists, teachers, social workers, and other community-engaged professionals operating within a deficit framework – and thus have been mostly overlooked in theory, research, and measurement models focusing on the effects of early adversity.

This error of omission has been damaging, not just because it perpetuates deficit-based thinking, but also because correcting the error – making hidden talents visible – can have a positive impact on adversity-exposed people. For example, randomized experiments have shown that guiding economically disadvantaged students toward recognizing that they have hidden talents as a result of their lived experiences, as well as exposing them to teachers who communicate that message, increases student motivation and academic persistence (Hernandez et al., 2021; Silverman et al., 2022). Such research underscores a defining characteristic of the hidden talents approach: that it communicates a novel, distinctive, and strength-based message that is the opposite of a deficit approach. In total, although adversity-mediated deficits are well-established, they are only part of the story; adversity-mediated adaptations, including development of hidden talents, are another part. Taken together, these different stress-mediated processes provide a well-rounded view of people who live with adversity.

The scientific goal of the hidden talents research program is to uncover a high-resolution map of the intact, or even enhanced, skills that emerge in harsh, unpredictable environments (i.e., *stress-adapted skills*), their development, and their manifestation in different contexts (Ellis et al., 2017; Ellis, Abrams et al., 2022; Frankenhuis & de Weerth, 2013; Frankenhuis, Young et al., 2020). Although skills that develop in response to adversity are not always socially desirable (e.g., skill at fighting), an assumption of the hidden talents model is that many stress-adapted skills have practical value that can be leveraged toward positive ends. Thus, the applied goal of the hidden talents framework is to work with positive stress-adapted skills to inform efforts and programs that potentiate success in education, employment, and civic life among adversity-exposed people.

1.1 Theoretical Foundations

The hidden talents model is rooted in a larger evolutionary-developmental framework focusing on developmental adaptation to stress (Belsky et al., 1991; Ellis & Del Giudice, 2014, 2019). In this framework, the term *adaptive* denotes the effect(s) of a trait on biological fitness (i.e., effects that were statistically linked to survival and reproduction over evolutionary time); it does not imply that a trait is socially desirable or conducive to subjective well-being. All adaptations have fitness costs as well as benefits. To be adaptive, a trait does not have to be cost free, but its benefits must have outweighed its costs over evolutionary history (such as when the benefits of persistent vigilance in a dangerous environment outweigh the costs of increased risk for stress-related mental illness). Such tradeoffs illustrate how early adversity can prompt the development of costly but adaptive strategies that increase fitness under stressful conditions (reviewed in Ellis & Del Giudice, 2014, 2019). This approach does not imply, however, that evolved developmental responses to adversity that paid off reproductively over human evolutionary history remain adaptive today – only that they remain operative.

We view the development of stress-adapted skills as functionally specialized for harsh, unpredictable environments (see Section 4). In turn, people who grow up under harsh, unpredictable conditions can be conceptualized as *stress-adapted*, rather than just "vulnerable" or "at-risk," even though there is marked variation in the outcomes of people exposed to such conditions, and even though the costs of developmental adaptation can result in genuine pathology or dysregulation. Stress has always been part of the human experience (Frankenhuis & Amir, 2022). Indeed, almost half of children in hunter–gatherer societies (the best model for human demographics before the agricultural revolution) die before reaching adulthood (e.g., Kaplan & Lancaster, 2003; Volk & Atkinson, 2013), making childhood – the time of the human life cycle when the force of selection is the strongest (Jones, 2009; Volk & Atkinson, 2008) – an intensive window for natural selection to operate on biobehavioral adaptations to stress. From an evolutionary-developmental perspective, therefore, stressful rearing conditions should not so much impair neurobiological systems as direct or regulate them toward patterns of functioning that are adaptive under stressful conditions (Belsky et al., 1991; Ellis & Del Giudice 2014, 2019), including development of stress-adapted skills. Following this logic, we use the term "stress-adapted" as shorthand for individuals or pheno-types that have (presumably) undergone developmental adaptation to stress, as mediated by adversity exposures. As discussed later in this section, such adaptations induce tradeoffs with potentially risky outcomes.

In the hidden talents framework, stress-adapted skills are considered to be a subset of all potential developmental adaptations to stress, with this subset limited to *skills* in which performance can be evaluated against objective benchmarks (i.e., agreed upon standards that indicate skill level), such as speed, accuracy, or success versus competition (e.g., athletic competition, artistic competition). This focus on criterion-referenced skills delimits the hidden talents domain and distinguishes it from other models focusing on developmental adaptation to stress (e.g., Belsky, 2019; Belsky et al., 1991; Del Giudice et al., 2011; Ellis et al., 2009; Nettle et al., 2013; Richters & Cicchetti, 1993). These other models focus on phenotypic outcomes that are not included in the hidden talents domain, such as physiological adaptations to stress (e.g., early puberty, accelerated biological aging); stress-adapted attitudes or values (e.g., hostile attribution bias, future discounting); and stress-adapted behavioral dispositions (e.g., insecure attachment, opportunistic interpersonal orientation, high impulsivity or aggression, early sex and reproduction). For example, hostile attribution bias (the tendency to systematically over-attribute hostile intent in ambiguous social situations) *does not* meet the definition of a skill, even if this bias is adaptive under harsh conditions, whereas the ability to accurately infer the intentions of others *does* meet this definition.[1] Other models

---

[1] By definition, skill level (proficiency) is determined by performance on the skill itself, not in relation to other variables. Imagine that two people, Liam and Charlotte, completed an emotion identification test. The test measures the ability to identify emotions in photographs of twenty faces. Liam judged the emotions accurately 90 percent of the time. Because Liam's proficiency at emotion identification is objectively benchmarked by his accuracy score, emotion identification meets the definition of a criterion-referenced skill. In addition, Liam is better than Charlotte at emotion identification. Charlotte only judged the emotions accurately 50 percent of the time. Further, Charlotte's errors were non-random; she systematically over-attributed negative emotions to the faces. Whereas Liam over-attributed negative emotions on one photograph, Charlotte over-attributed negative emotions on seven photographs. Charlotte thus scored higher than Liam on negative attribution bias. That is a bias, not a skill. Negative attribution bias is determined by how many items Charlotte got wrong (in a particular way), not by how many items she got right. Most critically, the question of whether negative attribution bias is adaptive is orthogonal to the question of whether it is a criterion-referenced skill. That Liam is better than Charlotte at emotion identification does not guarantee that he would do better than her, for example, at avoiding danger or negotiating a social conflict. In some situations, it may be more adaptive to be biased than accurate (see further discussion of this issue in Frankenhuis, Young, et al., 2020).

focusing on developmental adaptation to stress do not explicitly address criterion-referenced stress-adapted skills.

Despite this demarcation of the hidden talents domain, we expect stress-adapted skills to be associated with other developmental adaptations to stress; indeed, an evolutionary-developmental perspective clearly implies that such adaptations will be integrated and coherent. Along these lines, hidden talents have previously been conceptualized within a *life history framework* (Ellis et al., 2017). Life history theory addresses how organisms allocate their limited time and energy to the various activities – physical and cognitive development (growth), self-maintenance (health, survival), and mating and parenting (reproduction) – that comprise the life cycle (e.g., Del Giudice et al., 2015). Since all of these activities contribute to fitness, devoting time and energy to one will typically involve benefits as well as costs, engendering trade-offs between different fitness components. Such tradeoffs are central to developmental adaptations to stress – one system is diminished so that another can be enhanced or preserved – as evidenced by the growing empirical literature on the physical health costs of positive psychosocial adjustment in the context of childhood adversity (Hostinar & Miller, 2019). Developmental life history models have proposed that early exposures to harsh, unpredictable environments induce tradeoffs that increase the probability of developing "fast" life history strategies (e.g., earlier age at reproduction, more risky and aggressive behavior) that are, or once were, adaptive under stressful conditions (Del Giudice et al., 2015; Ellis et al., 2009). Tradeoffs incurred by a fast strategy include reduced health, vitality, and longevity (e.g., Belsky, 2019; Hill et al., 2016; Mell et al., 2018). Ellis et al. (2017) hypothesized that fast life history strategies may instantiate stress-adapted skills that are specialized for harsh, unpredictable environments.

Although suites of skills should be associated with different life history strategies, we do not expect that all individuals pursuing a particular strategy will have the same skill sets (Ellis et al., 2017). People should invest in skills and abilities that are relevant in their developmental context. For example, the concept of *environmental harshness,* which refers to external sources of morbidity and mortality that are relatively insensitive to the adaptive decisions and actions of the organism (Ellis et al., 2009), constitutes at least two distinct adaptive problems: harm imposed by other agents (threat) and insufficient environmental inputs (deprivation) (Ellis, Sheridan et al., 2022). A psychosocially neglected child experiencing deprivation and a physically abused child experiencing threat can be expected to develop overlapping skill sets that reflect the development of faster life history strategies in both family contexts (e.g., skill sets related to successfully attaining immediate rewards), but nonoverlapping skill sets that reflect differential exposures to threat versus deprivation.

Thus, there should be divergence in skills/abilities across individuals who differ in levels and types of childhood adversity exposures (Frankenhuis & de Weerth, 2013). Nonetheless, knowing what skills are adaptive in what contexts is not a trivial question (Frankenhuis, Young, et al., 2020). Addressing this question will require systematic cost-benefit analyses, ideally using formal mathematical models (see Frankenhuis et al., 2018), of the conditions under which different skills/abilities are adaptive.

A widespread idea in developmental psychopathology is that, although behaviors or physiological responses that develop in response to early adversity may have short-term survival advantages (e.g., heightened vigilance to threat), such behaviors and responses are poorly suited to more normative (e.g., safe, stable) environments and have long-term mental and physical health costs (e.g., McCrory & Viding, 2015). The hidden talents approach converges with this idea, but extends it by going beyond the notion of short-term advantages. Childhood adaptations to stress may eventuate in long-term adaptive changes in biobehavioral systems that regulate development over the life course (reviewed in Ellis & Del Giudice, 2014, 2019), including development of stress-adapted skills, despite the tradeoffs. Such complex developmental patterns underscore the need to examine adaptive and maladaptive processes together – and to model them in relation to each other – to more fully understand adversity-mediated variations in development (see Ellis, Sheridan et al., 2022; Frankenhuis, Young, et al., 2020, for extended discussion).

1.2 Working with Stress-Adapted Skills

Developmental adaptations to stress occur in adversity-exposed children. The question is what to do about it. A central goal of deficit-based approaches is to try to change these adaptations – to get children and youth from harsh, unpredictable environments to act, think, and feel more like children and youth from safe, stable environments. Changing people in this way, however, is an assimilation process, which invariably privileges dominant, middle-class values and behavior as the norm against which others are measured. Although intervening to change adversity-exposed children (such as by mitigating risk or ameliorating deficits) is a well-established approach, it is limited in important ways. Beyond the issue of assimilation, this approach assumes that healthy learning and development depend on rich learning experiences in safe, supportive environments (e.g., Learning Policy Institute & Turnaround for Children, 2021). Hundreds of millions of children worldwide, however, do not have access to these kinds of experiences and environments (e.g., Pinheiro, 2006; World Bank, 2018). How do we promote learning and development in these children? The simple answer – change the world that the children live in – is not always plausible or realistic. In many cases, it is necessary instead to work within the contexts of children's lives. That is where traditional approaches to intervention focusing on mitigating risk and ameliorating deficits fall short; they do not attempt to leverage – and thus cannot capitalize on – the unique strengths and abilities that develop in response to childhood adversity. Broadly speaking, intervention efforts may be stuck in a pattern of fighting against functional adaptations to adversity (Ellis et al., 2012, 2017).

In contrast, the hidden talents approach is to work with, rather than against, stress-adapted skills. The goal is to use the hidden talents of stress-adapted children and youth as building blocks for success, opening up opportunities that enable a wider range of individuals to achieve their full potential. *In advocating for this approach, it is important to emphasize that the goal is not to reinforce fast life history strategies or better prepare stress-adapted people to live their lives in harsh, unpredictable environments.* Rather, the goal is to enable people who have experienced significant adversity to use their hidden talents in positive ways – not only in domains valued by society, but in contexts that matter to them. Most critically, theory and research on hidden talents does not condone exposing children to adverse experiences that are obviously detrimental, such as abuse or neglect. Instead, observations of how neural and cognitive function adapt to harsh early circumstances may support a strengths-based approach to intervention that leverages stress-adapted skills (as detailed in the following sections on neural plasticity, educational strategies, social work, and resilience). This approach is consistent with the principle that strength-based social policy should be rooted in the experiences of the people targeted, congruent with their goals, and build on their skills and resources (Rapp et al., 2006).

We see these goals of the hidden talents approach as complementary to, rather than in conflict or competition with, more traditional intervention goals of mitigating risk and ameliorating deficits. If these traditional goals could be achieved, such as by eradicating poverty and other forms of childhood adversity and inequality globally, then the hidden talents approach would not be needed. That is a high bar, however, as every year hundreds of millions of children worldwide experience harm or threat of harm to their physical integrity (Pinheiro, 2006), and about 736 million people worldwide live in poverty (World Bank, 2018).

Short of that high bar, the hidden talents approach is a natural ally of more traditional intervention approaches. Taken together, the hidden talents and traditional approaches are well-positioned to advance balanced strategies – both building on stress-mediated adaptations and addressing stress-mediated vulnerabilities – for promoting positive development in the context of adversity. For example, it is well-documented that interventions designed to enhance social and emotional skills, improve IQ, improve academic performance and outcomes, build character traits (e.g., perseverance, sociability), reduce problematic behavior (e.g., bullying), and prevent mental and physical health problems (e.g., depression, obesity) are reasonably effective in children but decline in efficacy in adolescents (Heckman & Kautz, 2013; Yeager et al., 2018; for a meta-analysis, see Snyder et al., 2019). Yeager et al. (2018) propose that "traditional interventions fail when they do not align with adolescents' enhanced desire to feel respected and be accorded status" (p. 101). Because the hidden talents model recognizes and appreciates stress-adapted people for their skills, it aligns well with heightened sensitivity to status and respect among adolescents. In total, by working with rather than against stress-adapted skills – respecting the prior knowledge and abilities that diverse youth bring to the table – the hidden talents approach may help to fill a void where more traditional intervention approaches have foundered (see further discussion in Section 7).

1.3 Overview

In this Element, we survey the growing theoretical and empirical literature that has contributed to our understanding of hidden talents. Although we begin with a targeted empirical review of research on stress-adapted skills across social and cognitive domains (Section 2), our goal is to situate this research within a larger interdisciplinary framework. Drawing on cultural approaches to cognitive development, we propose that hidden talents are a form of adaptive intelligence that enables individuals to function within the constraints imposed by harsh, unpredictable environments (Section 4). We discuss the effects of growing up under such environmental conditions on the developing brain (Section 3). Changes in neurobehavioral phenotypes following early adversity provide evidence of developmental adaptations to stress in the form of hidden talents across multiple domains. Next we consider the implications of the hidden talents approach for policy and practice in two applied areas: school settings (Section 5), focusing on teaching and learning strategies that leverage stress-adapted skills, and the social work field (Section 6), focusing on intervention strategies for adjudicated youth and minority youth facing racial discrimination (including an initial discussion of racism-related stress within a hidden talents framework; Section 6.1). We provide a detailed discussion of implementation of the hidden talents approach in educational settings. We propose that hidden talents may be transferable and valuable for success in many normative contexts. Finally, we compare the hidden talents approach with contemporary resilience science (Section 7). While building on resilience science, we contend that theory and research on hidden talents has unique, innovative features and translational implications for stress-adapted children and youth.

2 Current Evidence for Hidden Talents

The study of hidden talents is an emerging research area; we know little and have much to learn. Current findings still need to be replicated, and we need to explore boundary conditions and generalizability. That said, the approach is promising. It has led to novel theory, empirical findings, and ideas for applications (Ellis et al., 2017; Ellis, Abrams et al., 2020; Frankenhuis & de Weerth, 2013). In this section, we highlight findings congruent with the concept of hidden talents, as well as mixed and negative evidence. These initial studies provide valuable clues and knowledge but are not conclusive.

2.1 The Specialization and Sensitization Hypotheses

Drawing on an evolutionary-developmental framework, Frankenhuis and de Weerth (2013) proposed that harsh, unpredictable environments do not exclusively impair cognitive abilities; instead, individuals become developmentally adapted ("specialized" and potentially enhanced) for solving problems that are ecologically relevant in such environments. Ellis et al. (2017) labelled this the *specialization hypothesis*. For example, in rapidly changing environments, heightened attention shifting may enable individuals to take advantage of fleeting opportunities, even if frequent shifting interferes with sustained attention (Mittal et al., 2015). A corollary of the specialization hypothesis is the *sensitization hypothesis* (Ellis et al., 2017), which proposes that advantages in cognitive function among people who grow up under harsh, unpredictable conditions (as per the specialization hypothesis) manifest primarily under currently stressful conditions (i.e., earlier-life experiences *sensitize* later responses to stress). For example, stress-adapted youth may be advantaged at attention shifting under conditions of current stress and uncertainty, but not in benign, nonthreatening circumstances (Mittal et al., 2015). The specialization and sensitization hypotheses are depicted in Figure 1.

The sensitization hypothesis assumes that the day-to-day experiences and circumstances of stress-adapted individuals are qualitatively different from those of individuals who grew up under safe, stable conditions; accordingly, testing stress-adapted children and youth under standard laboratory conditions may disadvantage them by not allowing them to show their abilities in context (i.e., their abilities to solve problems and achieve goals within their local ecology; see Section 4). Stress-adapted children and youth may instead perform

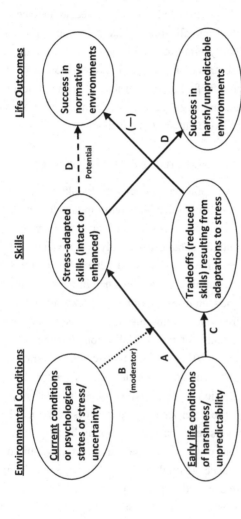

Environmental Conditions

Current conditions or psychological states of stress/uncertainty

Early life conditions of harshness/unpredictability

B (moderator)

A

C

Skills

Stress-adapted skills (intact or enhanced)

Tradeoffs (reduced skills) resulting from adaptations to stress

D Potential

Life Outcomes

Success in normative environments

Success in harsh/unpredictable environments

D

(−)

Figure 1 The hidden talents model. All paths are positive, except where indicated by (−). A. Specialization hypothesis (Frankenhuis & de Weerth, 2013): Developmental exposures to harsh/unpredictable environments enhance skills for solving problems that are ecologically relevant in such environments. B. Sensitization hypothesis (Ellis et al., 2017): Hypothesized advantages in cognitive abilities – stress-adapted skills – result from the interaction between early life and current conditions (i.e., developmentally honed skills are manifest primarily under current conditions or psychological states of stress/uncertainty). C. Costs of adaptation: Developmental exposures to harsh/unpredictable environments can induce tradeoffs that undermine certain skill sets. D. Potential outcomes: The central applied question of the hidden talents model is whether stress-adapted skills that enable individuals to function in harsh/unpredictable environments can be leveraged to promote success in normative contexts (dashed line), such as schools and work places.

certain tasks better in settings that do not attempt to minimize the reality of daily stressors and uncertainties. We discuss this issue in depth in Section 5.

The specialization and sensitization hypotheses draw on a larger body of evidence from nonhuman animal studies. Consistent with the specialization hypothesis (Figure 1), research in birds and rodents indicates that early experiences of adversity can improve specific forms of attention, perception, learning and memory, and problem-solving that are ecologically relevant under stressful conditions (reviewed in Ellis et al., 2017; Eyck et al., 2019). Further, as per the sensitization hypothesis (Figure 1), some of these abilities are manifest only in currently stressful contexts, where they would provide the greatest advantages. That is, some enhancements occur only when developmental specializations are activated by current experiences or psychological states of stress/uncertainty. For instance, when tested under basal conditions, rodent pups that received low maternal care showed lower performance in a contextual fear-conditioning paradigm than pups that received high maternal care. However, when tested under stressful conditions (characterized by elevated glucocorticoid levels typical of an active stress response), the low-maternal care pups showed enhanced performance (Bagot et al., 2009; Champagne et al., 2008).

In order to evaluate tests of both the specialization and sensitization hypotheses, we review research on both childhood and current experiences of adversity, and on how the effects of adversity interact with experimentally manipulated psychological states. We exclude research, however, that examines only the effects of experimentally manipulated states (e.g., scarcity mindsets), without considering childhood or current experiences of adversity. In our view, manipulated contextual effects on social and cognitive skills, independent of lived experiences, are outside of the purview of the hidden talents model.

2.2 Identifying and Remembering Negative Emotions and Experiences

Initial human studies of hidden talents in humans focused mainly on threat and negative experiences. Early-life experiences involving actual harm or threat of harm to a child, including direct victimization experiences (e.g., physical abuse), as well as those witnessed by the child (e.g., violence between caregivers), alter salience detection and aversive learning in ways that facilitate rapid identification of potential danger in the environment and mobilize defensive responses (McLaughlin et al., 2014, 2019; McLaughlin & Lambert, 2017). These threat-mediated processes support development of specific hidden talents. As this literature is nuanced and complex, we present only a selection of key findings, focusing on identifying and remembering negative emotions and experiences.

In a systematic review, da Silva Ferreira and colleagues (2014) concluded that children who have experienced maltreatment (including both abuse and neglect) tend to be less accurate in global facial expression tasks while showing "greater reactivity, response bias, and electrophysiological activation of specific brain areas in response to faces expressing negative emotions, especially anger" (p. 1). Consistent with having specialized skills, physically abused children may be more accurate than non-maltreated children at identifying angry (but not other) facial expressions from degraded pictures (Pollak, 2008), at recalling distracting aggressive stimuli (e.g., knives, guns; Rieder & Cicchetti, 1989), and at remembering a doctor who performed an invasive examination (Eisen et al., 2007). Such effects are apparently dose-dependent: children who have experienced more severe abuse identified anger the earliest from the degraded stimuli (Pollak et al., 2009). A recent meta-analysis found that children exposed to severe acute/chronic stress of any kind (specific dimensions of adversity were not analyzed) had faster reaction times, but average recognition accuracy, in response to both angry and sad faces (Saarinen et al., 2021).[2] At the same time, maltreated children may display an attribution bias toward anger, ascribing this emotion to situations where it is not fitting (Pollak et al., 2000; see also Frankenhuis & Bijlstra, 2018). An integrative review concluded that maltreatment enhances attention and memory for negative emotionally laden or stressful information in most people, but results in attention and memory deficits for negative or traumatic experiences in others (Goodman et al., 2010). Future research is needed to determine what factors regulate these individual differences.

2.3 Reward-Oriented Choices and Problem-Solving

Other developmental research suggests that children exposed to early adversity (e.g., poverty, maternal disengagement, unstable family environments) develop enhanced problem-solving skills for detecting/extracting fleeting or unpredictable rewards from the environment (Davies et al., 2022; Li et al., 2021; Sturge-Apple et al., 2017; Suor et al., 2017). Such skills apparently trade off against decreased performance on explicit measures of higher-order cognitive functioning (e.g., IQ, working memory, abstract problem-solving; Davies et al., 2022; Suor et al., 2017). The extent to which the positive side of this tradeoff – enhanced skill among stress-adapted children at securing resources under

---

[2] For young children, tested before age 5, early adversity was associated with lower accuracy rates in response to both happy and fearful faces (Saarinen et al., 2021). The meaning of these specific age x accuracy interactions, involving both early timing of exposure and assessment, is unclear.

transient, changing conditions – is based on reward-oriented problem-solving versus sensitivity to punishment is currently unknown.

Maltreated children and adolescents tend to be more loss-avoidant than their non-maltreated peers (e.g., choosing safe options on a risky decision-making task, making risky choices to avoid losses; Guyer et al., 2006; Weller et al., 2015). Physically abused children are also more likely than nonabused children to respond to probabilistic positive feedback (rewards in an associative learning paradigm) as if it were largely random or unreliable (Hanson et al., 2017; see also Lloyd et al., 2022). Further, children experiencing low-income and economic marginalization tend to have more of a here-and-now orientation – taking advantage of opportunities to gain high rewards now despite a net loss over time – even when they consciously understand that the higher initial rewards result in greater punishments in the long run (Delgado et al., 2022). Although these decision-making and learning strategies have been interpreted from a deficit perspective (Guyer et al., 2006; Hanson et al., 2017; Weller et al., 2015), such strategies may be adaptive in adverse ecologies, where stress-adapted children have limited "reserve capacity" (Gallo & Matthews, 2003), making losses especially costly, and where rewards are unpredictable. The notion of adaptive risk-taking and response biases in the context of adversity is discussed further in Section 3.

2.4 Attunement to Other People and Social Information/ Relationships

Another set of studies suggests that people from lower-socioeconomic status (SES) backgrounds display greater attunement to other people and social information/relationships. Lower-SES ecologies tend to be relatively harsh and unpredictable. People inhabiting such ecologies are not only more likely to face resource scarcity, food insecurity, physical dangers, fleeting opportunities, and threats without warning, but also have relatively little personal control over these environmental conditions (Kraus et al., 2012). Developmental adaptation to lower-SES environments, therefore, may preferentially regulate attention toward "external, uncontrollable social forces and other individuals who influence one's life outcomes" (Kraus et al., 2012, p. 546) and involve other-oriented emotion and behavior. Such contextualist tendencies may function to promote behavioral prediction/management in a context of low resources and social rank.

Research in this area has focused on adults rather than children. Consistent with the contextualist hypothesis, people experiencing lower-SES conditions apparently show greater empathic accuracy, compassion, and attentiveness to others (reviewed in Kraus et al., 2012; Piff et al., 2018); exhibit better incidental memory for faces (Dietze et al., 2022); develop a more nuanced understanding of uncertainty and change in social relationships (Brienza & Grossmann, 2017); do better at working collaboratively to achieve collective outcomes (Dittmann et al., 2020); and display greater skill at assuming the visual perspective of another person (Dietze & Knowles, 2020), categorizing perceptually ambiguous groups of people (Bjornsdottir et al., 2017), decoding nonverbal cues such as facial expressions of emotion (Bjornsdottir et al., 2017; Dietze & Knowles, 2020; Kraus et al., 2010; Monroy et al., 2022), and signaling their emotions to others (Monroy et al., 2022). In one study, postinstitutionalized adopted youth were more accurate in choosing whether to trust their peers, and were more sensitive to both social reciprocation and defection, than never-institutionalized nonadopted youth (Pitula et al., 2017).

Research in this domain has used different methodologies. The most intensive approach involves laboratory studies of social interactions. This kind of study, while involving relatively small samples, is likely the most ecologically valid because social cues are communicated through multiple sensory channels via real-life interactions between participants (e.g., a mock job interview, teasing interactions with a friend). In these laboratory studies, both *subjective* perceptions of lower social class (an individual's sense of their social position relative to others) and *objective* resource-based measures of lower social class (e.g., income, education) predict greater attunement to other people and social information/relationships (Kraus et al., 2010, 2011; Kraus & Keltner, 2009; Stellar et al., 2012). By contrast, in studies using online recruitment and testing of participants, the effects of subjective and objective social class are divergent. These studies have employed relatively large numbers of online workers to complete computer-based tasks, focusing mostly on emotion recognition. The most commonly used task has been Reading the Mind in the Eyes (Baron-Cohen et al., 2001), which tests the ability to identify emotions based on greyscale images of the eyes. Whereas online research using subjective measures of social class has documented consistent associations between lower perceived SES and greater accuracy in recognizing emotions/correctly inferring the emotions of others (Bjornsdottir et al., 2017; Dietze & Knowles, 2020; Monroy et al., 2022; Schmalor & Heine, 2022), online research using objective measures of social class has either found null effects or that people with higher objective SES are better at recognizing and discriminating between emotions (Bjornsdottir et al., 2017; Deveney et al., 2018). This duality has been established across well-powered, preregistered studies (Deveney et al., 2018; Dietze & Knowles, 2020). Subjective social class may be especially relevant to understanding attunement to social information/relationships because it reflects one's internalization or personal conceptualization of their position in social hierarchies.

2.5 Executive Functions

Within the hidden talents framework, a substantial focus of research has been on specific components of executive functioning – especially attention shifting and working-memory updating – that theoretically should enable individuals to take advantage of fleeting opportunities, avoid unpredictable threats, and update changing information in chaotic/unstable environments. One set of studies found that adults who reported experiencing more unpredictable home environments while growing up displayed enhanced attention shifting (efficient switching between different tasks) but reduced inhibitory control (deliberate overriding of dominant responses), but only when tested in an experimentally induced context of economic decline/uncertainty (Mittal et al., 2015). That people displayed enhanced attention shifting specifically when put in a context that was reminiscent of the unpredictable environments in which they grew up is consistent with the sensitization hypothesis. In another study, which did not manipulate psychological states, adults who had greater lifetime trauma exposure were better at dynamically regulating cognitive control in response to changing contexts (Steudte-Schmiedgen et al., 2014).

Subsequent research conducted with children has tested for the effects of various forms of childhood adversity on attention-shifting performance. None of this work has included experimental manipulations of psychological state; thus, it has only tested the specialization hypothesis. In a sample enriched for caregiver instability (e.g., institutional placements, foster care history), more caregiver changes – a key indicator of environmental unpredictability – were associated with heightened attention-shifting abilities, but reduced inhibitory control, in school-age children (Fields et al., 2021). Thus, high levels of unpredictability predicted the same cognitive tradeoff documented in Mittal et al. (2015).[3] Likewise, in a diverse sample of middle school students

---

[3] Cognitive systems are constrained by tradeoffs between "separately advantageous but conflicting traits" (Del Giudice & Crespi, 2018, p. 56). For example, better attention shifting apparently trades off against worse inhibitory control in six-year-olds (i.e., these two traits are negatively correlated; Blackwell et al., 2014). Although a negative correlation between traits is consistent with the presence of a tradeoff (meaning that an increase in one trait causes a decrease in the other), the absence of a negative correlation does not indicate the absence of such a tradeoff. Correlations are often confounded, as in the case when different individuals in a study population differ in physical condition, access to resources, social/cognitive stimulation, etc. (e.g., Bolund, 2020; Ellis et al., 2009). In this case, the person who is in good physical condition, has ready access to resources, and inhabits a socially/cognitively enriched environment may develop better cognitive abilities across conflicting traits (e.g., attention shifting and inhibitory control) than another person who is in poor condition, has meager resources, and is socially/cognitively

(about half of whom were economically disadvantaged), children who had more exposure to environmental unpredictability or violence while growing up displayed small advantages in attention-shifting performance (Young et al., 2022). Exploratory analyses showed that this effect was driven by the child's overall perception of family unpredictability (the same measure used in Mittal et al., 2015) and not by number of caregiver transitions (which was low). In Fields et al. (2021), experiencing zero versus one caregiver transition was not linked to attention-shifting performance or inhibitory control; only children who experienced multiple caregiver transitions showed better attention shifting and worse inhibitory control. Finally, in a Nigerian study, children raised in orphanages or foster care were compared with a control group raised by their biological parent(s) (Nweze et al., 2021). There were no differences between the two groups in either attention shifting or inhibitory control. Data were not collected, however, on the number of times children had been placed into different institutions/foster homes; thus, we do not know whether children who experienced multiple institutional/foster care placements displayed the same apparent tradeoff between attention shifting and inhibitory control that was documented in Fields et al. (2021).

Another set of studies found that adults who reported experiencing more unpredictable home environments while growing up displayed enhanced working memory updating (tracking changing information; replacing older information that is no longer relevant with new, updated information), but reduced working memory retrieval/capacity (storing and maintaining important information, even during interference), but only when tested in an experimentally induced context of economic decline/uncertainty (Young et al., 2018). Thus, again, enhanced cognitive performance in one domain apparently traded off against worse performance in another domain. As with the attention shifting findings discussed earlier in this section (Mittal et al., 2015), these results are consistent with the sensitization hypothesis. When participants were tested under neutral conditions, individuals who reported higher levels of childhood unpredictability displayed worse working memory updating. Subsequent research conducted with middle school students tested for the effects of various forms of childhood adversity on working memory updating performance (Young et al., 2022). As this research did not involve manipulation of current

---

deprived. These disparities can generate positive correlations between people in cognitive traits that are in fact negatively correlated within a given person. One way around this confound is to experimentally manipulate environmental conditions. In research discussed in this section (Mittal et al., 2015; Young et al., 2018), the same experimentally manipulated environmental exposure moved "separately advantageous but conflicting traits" in opposite directions, indicating cognitive tradeoffs in response to the environmental exposure.

psychological states, it only tested for specialization. The preregistered goal of this research was to test the hypothesis that hidden talents were more likely to emerge when testing content/stimuli were ecologically relevant to adversity-exposed children (e.g., when working memory updating tasks used familiar real-world stimuli such as a city bus or a $5 bill rather than abstract stimuli such as circles and triangles). As in much past research on executive functioning (e.g., Ursache & Noble, 2016), children exposed to higher levels of poverty and violence (but not unpredictability) displayed worse working memory updating when the assessment was based on abstract stimuli; however, that performance gap was essentially eliminated when the assessment of working memory updating was based on ecologically relevant stimuli (Young et al., 2022). These results concur with Rifkin-Graboi et al. (2021), which found that preschool girls exposed to more caregiver adversity were more accurate on relational memory for socioemotional stimuli, but less accurate for nonsocioemotional stimuli.

Other work testing for sensitization effects on learning and memory has focused on socioeconomic disadvantage or crime exposure. Under primed conditions of high financial demand, people from lower-SES backgrounds displayed enhanced procedural learning (acquiring stimulus-response associations) but reduced performance on cognitive functions that rely more heavily on working memory (Dang et al., 2016; Mani et al., 2013; but see González-Arango et al., 2022). Among children residing in high-poverty, high-crime neighborhoods, living in proximity to a recent violent crime predicted faster but marginally less accurate cognitive processing, suggesting a shift toward more automatic responding (McCoy et al., 2015). This emerging body of work on potential enhancements in cognitive abilities needs to be more systematically integrated with the well-developed program of research in neuroscience showing that stress affects different memory systems in different ways. High levels of acute stress may cause a shift from top-down explicit (hippocampal-prefrontal dependent) memory systems to bottom-up procedural (striatum-dependent) systems (Leonard et al., 2015; Schwabe & Wolf, 2013; Vogel et al., 2016). Could this shift explain the finding that, on procedural memory tasks, people currently living in poverty perform just as well (Leonard et al., 2015), or even better (Dang et al., 2016), than higher-SES individuals?

2.6 Childhood versus Current Adversity Exposures

An emerging literature has examined the effects of both childhood adversity and current adversity on stress-adapted skills. There is mixed evidence regarding the effects of early versus current violence exposure on the ability to memorize the structure of social environments. Whereas more *current* exposure to violence in adults predicted intact or even enhanced memory for social-dominance relationships, retrospectively reported *childhood* exposure to violence predicted impaired memory for social-dominance relationships (Frankenhuis, de Vries et al., 2020). This contrast between current and childhood experiences raises a central question for the hidden talents model: To what extent does enhanced performance of stress-adapted individuals, whether in children or adults, depend on developmentally calibrated traits (e.g., early biological embedding of adversity) versus current experiences/states? This question is visually depicted in Figure 1 in relation the specialization and sensitization hypotheses. In a study of adults who did not report any significant traumatic experiences in childhood, trauma-exposed criminal scene investigator police, relative to a control group, showed enhanced performance on a simple discrimination task in the presence of high-intensity aversive pictures (e.g., facial expressions of fear) but impaired performance in the presence of low-intensity aversive pictures (Levy-Gigi et al., 2016); moreover, greater on-the-job trauma exposure was associated with better performance in the high-intensity condition ($r = 0.42$). Thus, as in Frankenhuis, de Vries et al. (2020), current experiences in adulthood appeared to calibrate stress-adapted skills.

2.7 Conclusion

In conclusion, people who grow up under adverse conditions might not perform worse on all social and cognitive tasks; rather, compared with people from more stable or supportive environments, their performance may be enhanced on tasks that reflect significant challenges within the constraints imposed by harsh, unpredictable environments (Ellis et al., 2017; Frankenhuis & de Weerth, 2013). In this section, we reviewed a range of potential hidden talents: Identifying and remembering negative emotions and experiences (e.g., rapid identification of potential danger), reward-oriented choices and problem-solving (e.g., detecting/extracting fleeting or unpredictable rewards from the environment), attunement to other people and social relationships/information (e.g., empathic accuracy, emotion recognition), collaborative abilities (discussed further in Section 5.1), and executive function components (e.g., attention shifting, working memory updating). This empirical literature on hidden talents affords a striking contrast to the broader developmental literature, which has emphasized deficits in people with significant exposures to adversity (though with notable exceptions such as developmental resilience models; see Section 7). Nonetheless, the current evidence base for hidden talents is limited, key findings still need to be replicated, and important theoretical and methodological issues remain (see Frankenhuis, Young, et al., 2020; Szepsenwol, 2022). Here we discuss three key issues that, if addressed in future research, should provide the foundation for a more coherent and reliable body of knowledge about hidden talents, their development, and their manifestation in different contexts.

2.7.1 Levels and Types of Adversity

First, the hidden talents research program needs to better delineate how different levels and types of adversity, whether objectively or subjectively experienced, relate to stress-adapted skills. In terms of *levels* of adversity, research on hidden talents needs to adequately sample the range/severity of early-life experiences. For example, the same measure of perceived family unpredictability (when completed under neutral conditions) was unrelated to attention shifting in relatively low-risk college student samples (Mittal et al., 2015) but predicted better attention shifting in a more diverse middle school sample (Young et al., 2022). Likewise, in samples of children with relatively high adversity exposure, multiple caregiving transitions (but not a single transition) predicted heightened attention shifting (Fields et al., 2021). Further, unusually high levels of parental anger predicted the ability to accurately recognize angry faces based on minimal cues (Pollak et al., 2009). In terms of *types* of adversity, theory and research on hidden talents needs to address the effects of specific dimensions of early experience. For example, threatening experiences during childhood alter the development of neural networks that underlie salience detection and aversive learning in ways that facilitate rapid identification of potential danger in the environment, including enhanced skill at detecting anger; by contrast, childhood experiences of deprivation are not linked to these alterations in emotional processing and associated neural circuits (reviewed in Ellis, Sheridan et al., 2022; McLaughlin et al., 2019). Finally, both objective and subjective experiences of adversity need to be tested in relation to hidden talents, as clearly demonstrated by the literature on SES and emotion recognition. Subjective assessments may be especially important in more normative samples without severe adversity exposures.

2.7.2 Effects of Current Conditions and Psychological States

Second, the hidden talents research program needs to more systematically consider the effects of current conditions and psychological states on stress-adapted skills. Both childhood and adult experiences of adversity are associated with variation in hidden talents. But we need to learn more about how early and current adversity exposures interact – both with each other and with current psychological states – to regulate hidden talents (Frankenhuis, Young, et al., 2020). Work testing the sensitization hypothesis has shown that young adults who grew up in unpredictable home environments display enhanced attention shifting and working-memory updating when in an experimentally induced mindset of stress/uncertainty (Mittal et al., 2015; Young et al., 2018). That may be just the tip of the iceberg. A growing experimental literature in children has shown that performance on executive function tasks is sensitive to context (e.g., Miller-Cotto et al., 2022), such as manipulated information about peer group performance (Doebel & Munakata, 2018), contextual cues relevant to task goals (Freier et al., 2021), and task administration in classroom versus one-on-one settings (Obradović et al., 2018). Applied work on hidden talents, such as in educational settings (see Section 5), would greatly benefit from knowing how such contextual effects interact with both early-life adversity and recent adversity exposures. Most importantly, experimental work on hidden talents has shown that manipulations of future economic decline/uncertainty induce apparent tradeoffs in cognitive abilities (e.g., in working memory updating versus working memory retrieval/capacity) that go in different directions for people who report different levels of childhood unpredictability (Mittal et al., 2015; Young et al., 2018). Mapping out these kinds of sensitization effects, and especially the resulting cognitive tradeoffs in diverse populations, is a critical direction for future research. Such interactions would be best studied using research designs that compare not only performance across individuals, but also different abilities within the same person (enhanced vs. nonenhanced abilities) across different conditions (e.g., experimental manipulation vs. control) (Frankenhuis, Young, et al., 2020).

2.7.3 Ecological Validity

Third, the hidden talents research program needs to more carefully test for stress-adapted skills in ecologically valid contexts. A critical question raised by the hidden talents model is: Do differences in social/cognitive skills between people with different experiences of adversity reflect disparities in mental abilities (as per deficit models)? Or do these differences result partly – or even largely – from a mismatch between the social/cognitive skills of stress-adapted people and (a) the kinds of skills that are usually assessed by researchers and/or (b) the ways/contexts in which those skills are assessed? We discuss this question in depth in Section 4 and Section 5. Whatever the ultimate answer to this question, we expect that hidden talents will more clearly emerge (a) when researchers test for theoretically relevant stress-adapted skills and (b) when test settings and the content of testing materials are more ecologically relevant and concrete (Ellis et al., 2017; Frankenhuis & de Weerth, 2013; Young et al., 2022). In short, researchers need to capture the contexts in which hidden talents are expected to unfold.

Typical cognitive tests use abstract content that is largely detached from the real world. Such abstract materials may disadvantage people whose childhood experiences involve less abstract, analytical problem-solving (see Section 4). As reviewed in Section 2.5, research on hidden talents that has replaced sterile testing materials with ecologically relevant content from the real world has shown some evidence of reducing, eliminating, or even reversing deficits among adversity-exposed children and adults (Frankenhuis, de Vries et al., 2020; Rifkin-Graboi et al., 2021; Young et al., 2022). Research in this domain has generated complex findings, however, which we discuss in more detail in Section 5. The next step will be to measure stress-adapted skills in more ecological ways that go beyond standard lab tasks (even if those tasks use ecologically valid stimuli or content) – as standard lab tasks may not capture underlying processes that mechanistically support real-world functioning (Doebel, 2020). As a starting point, Doebel (2020, p. 952) suggests that "instead of asking children to inhibit pressing a button on a screen, they could be asked to inhibit touching attractive unattended toys on display for a period of time or to periodically switch between practical tasks." One real-world example is research asking shoppers in grocery stores to recall the price of items in their cart (Wakefield & Inman, 1993); lower-income shoppers were able to report prices more accurately.[4] In total, using ecologically valid content, especially in the context of naturalistic or real-world tasks, may be needed to fully uncover hidden talents.

Finally, the foregoing review of current evidence for hidden talents does not directly address the right side of Figure 1, which represents applications: the hypothesized relations between stress-adapted skills and success in different environmental contexts. The dashed line depicts the *potential* role of stress-adapted skills in promoting success in normative contexts – a role that has not been empirically tested. As discussed in the remaining sections of this Element, describing and evaluating this applied role is critical to guiding efforts and programs for leveraging hidden talents in ways that potentiate success among adversity-exposed people.

3 Neural Plasticity Enables the Development of Hidden Talents

The hidden talents approach aligns with emerging neuroscience research on developmental adaptation to stress. The study of neural plasticity, at its core, concerns developmental adaptation to the environment. Indeed, the human

---

[4] Even in studies using less ecologically grounded methods (e.g., questionnaires), meta-analyses have shown that lower income levels are associated with greater price knowledge and better price recall accuracy (Estelami & Lehmann, 2001; Estelami et al., 2001).

brain has been described as the ultimate organ of adaptation, changing in structure and function with experience, including developmental exposures to stress (Kolb & Gibb, 2014; McEwen, 2009; Teicher et al., 2016).

Human brain development begins prenatally yet continues for at least another two to three decades (e.g., Fox et al., 2010; Tottenham, 2020). This protracted period of immaturity supports extended learning from and about the environment, providing numerous opportunities to developmentally adapt to local environmental conditions. This process tends to promote adaptation in context. That is, children tend to develop in ways that are adaptive within the constraints of their lived environments, even if the early social-emotional context is harsh or unpredictable (reviewed in Ellis & Del Giudice, 2019). Such developmental adaptations are reflected in brain structure and function (see especially D'angiulli et al., 2012). A growing literature on the neuroscience of adversity highlights divergent patterns of neurobiological development in circuits involving the amygdala, prefrontal cortex, striatum, and hippocampus following early exposures to adversity (e.g., McDermott et al., 2019; McLaughlin et al., 2019; Teicher et al., 2016; Tooley et al., 2021). In turn, neurobiological phenotypes associated with early adversity – even if such phenotypes reflect the outcome of adaptive developmental processes – tend to correlate with outcomes that are considered undesirable by normative standards and may be costly to the individual, such as internalizing and externalizing behaviors or disadvantages on standard measures of neurocognitive functioning such as language, memory, and executive function (Farah, 2017; Jenness et al., 2021; McDermott et al., 2019; Teicher et al., 2016; Ursache & Noble, 2016).

As discussed in Section 1, data linking early adversity to risk for atypical patterns of brain development and associated outcomes have reinforced prevailing deficit models. Such deficit-based thinking assumes that children raised in supportive and well-resourced environments tend to develop normally and manifest so-called "optimal" trajectories and outcomes. Notions of "normal" and "optimal" in this context all-too-often imply that the natural course of human development, from youth to later in life, is to become more secure, autonomous, self-regulating, hardworking, etc. According to this deficit perspective, children exposed to early adversities are at risk for developmental dysfunction, dysregulation, and disorder – the opposite of "normal" and "optimal" – leading to problem behaviors that are destructive to themselves and others (see Ellis et al., 2012; Ellis, Sheridan et al., 2022).

The fault in this reasoning is that brain and behavioral development are best understood as adaptations to a child's ecological niche on relatively short timescales (Johnson et al., 2015; Nketia et al., 2021). As per life history theory, development instantiates a chain of resource-allocation decisions, favoring investment in some developmental domains at a cost to others. These tradeoffs shape phenotypes in ways that historically enhanced expected fitness within the opportunities and constraints of a given environment (Ellis & Del Giudice, 2019). As stated by Noble and colleagues (2021, p. 1488): "Neurodevelopmental differences after adversity frequently represent the expected and contextually appropriate response of the developing brain." This viewpoint converges with a basic assumption of the hidden talents model: Skills and other traits that are advantageous – and thus valued – in normative (i.e., safe, stable) contexts may not be optimal or adaptive in contexts of adversity. Accordingly, there is no single "normal" or "optimal" phenotype; developmental adaptation to one ecological niche may result in mismatch to another (see Section 4). Stated differently: "Within normative variability, there is no good brain or bad brain. There is only human diversity" (Nketia et al., 2021, p. 2). Within this normative range, notions of typical and atypical brain development reflect dominant cultural values and ideology. Recent data showing that brain structure and function related to cognitive performance may differ by SES (Ellwood-Lowe et al., 2021; Leonard et al., 2019) concur with this idea.

That said, children who experience significant early-life adversity are still at risk for relatively poor cognitive, emotional, and neurobiological outcomes by normative group standards and measures (e.g., Duncan et al., 2017; Ursache & Noble, 2016). These disparities, which deserve our utmost attention, are one part of the story. But developmental adaptations to stress are another part. Accurate characterization of such adaptations – including hidden talents – has been obscured by dominant cultural values and ideology, which do not "see" stress-adapted skills. Research on neurobiological adaptations to harsh environments has begun to correct this oversight, elucidating developmental processes leading to stress-adapted skills. Although this neurobiological research should be seen as a promissory note, as it was not designed to test for hidden talents and mostly focuses on potential short-term survival advantages (as opposed to longer-term adaptive calibration), it provides an initial picture of the neural bases of emerging stress-adapted skills under highly stressful early life conditions.

3.1 Adversity-Driven Brain Plasticity

Amygdala hyperactivity is frequently associated with child maltreatment (see Hein & Monk, 2017, for a meta-analysis) and has been observed following various forms of poor caregiving in rodent, monkey, and human models (Callaghan et al., 2014). For example, amygdala hyperactivity to negative emotional cues has been observed in children following exposures to different forms abuse and neglect (e.g., Bogdan et al., 2012; Gee et al., 2013; Puetz et al., 2020). Although the amygdala plays a central role in internalizing problems associated with early-life stress, high amygdala reactivity following early adversity has been linked to better goal-directed behavior when the goal is compatible with threat detection (Silvers et al., 2017). Specifically, previously institutionalized youth with higher amygdala reactivity exhibited both higher anxiety symptoms and better performance (i.e., faster search times) when spatially locating fearful faces in an array of neutral ones.

A substantial research literature has also linked amygdala volume to early-life stress, though the findings are complex (see McLaughlin et al., 2019). Teicher et al. (2016) suggest that early increases in amygdala volume following early-life stress may sensitize the amygdala to future stressors, resulting in later-occurring amygdala atrophy. This hypothesis received empirical support in a recent longitudinal study of youth with histories of separation/abandonment and institutional care (VanTieghem et al., 2021). This finding highlights the importance of considering development when reviewing the literature on neural phenotypes following early adversity, as these trajectories may be informative for models of developmental adaptation. One study compared previously institutionalized children who spent more time in orphanage care (late adoption) with peers who spent less time in orphanage care (early adoption) and a never-institutionalized comparison group (Tottenham et al., 2010). Children who were adopted at later ages had larger amygdala volumes, were biased toward false alarm errors when responding to negatively valenced faces in an inhibitory control task, and experienced increased anxiety. The false alarms – specifically in response to facial expressions of negative emotions such as fear and anger – could be interpreted as enhanced threat sensitivity, which generally characterizes previously institutionalized children (Gunnar & Reid, 2019). The larger picture that emerged from these two studies (Silvers et al., 2017; Tottenham et al., 2010) was that early institutional care, as mediated by morphologic and neurofunctional changes in the amygdala, regulated children's development toward heightened threat vigilance, which was expressed phenotypically in terms of stress-adapted skills (faster search times), response biases (false alarm errors), and personality dispositions (anxiety). These phenotypic responses to early-life stress were coherent and integrated; over evolutionary time, such responses may have promoted survival in childhood environments characterized by high levels of caregiver deprivation and other forms of adversity.

Higher anxiety levels in individuals with a history of institutional care are also associated with decision-making strategies that appear specialized to harsh, unpredictable conditions. For example, when deciding whether to *explore* environmental cues (increasing both the opportunity for larger rewards and the threat of punishment) or *exploit* them (by securing a small but reward-promising outcome), children with a history of institutional caregiving use more exploitative strategies relative to peers without such a history (Humphreys et al., 2015; Kopetz et al., 2019; Loman et al., 2014). Humphreys et al. (2015) found that the exploitive strategy increased youths' earnings as a function of context: It proved detrimental under forgiving experimental conditions (when punishing feedback was slow to come), but beneficial when conditions became harsh (i.e., when parameters of the task changed to hasten punishment).

Another behavior commonly observed in children with a history of institutional care, and more broadly in fostered populations (Love et al., 2015), is disinhibited social engagement (DSE). DSE is characterized by age-inappropriate approach behavior and/or intimacy directed at unfamiliar adults including strangers. Once children are in a stable caregiving environment, this behavior can be disturbing to families and put the child in danger (even though exposure to high-quality caregiving may mitigate DSE; reviewed in Love et al., 2015). Functional neuroimaging has shown that DSE behaviors in children with a history of institutional care are correlated with the amygdala's indiscriminate response to both parents and strangers (Olsavsky et al., 2013). Importantly, this lack of differential responding to parents and strangers was the result of previously institutionalized youth exhibiting overly heightened responses to the strangers. Although this behavior is highly unusual under conditions of typical caregiving, it may be an adaptive response to early neglect (Lawler et al., 2014) in that it promotes caregiving responses from adults (even if this behavior is associated with relatively poor outcomes later in life; Gleason et al., 2011; Guyon-Harris et al., 2019). For a young child who experiences caregiving neglect and/or instability, maintaining openness to nonparental adults is a potentially important survival skill, which may function to recruit potential new/replacement caregivers. DSE behavior may thus be an enhanced sociability skill in young children that develops in response to low-quality caregiving. In this context, the amygdala may develop in a way that maintains strong motivational value representations for unfamiliar adults in anticipation of future caregiving instability.

3.2 Stress-Acceleration Hypothesis

Motivated by a growing animal literature identifying accelerated development of emotion-related neurobiology following early life stress, Callaghan and Tottenham (2016) proposed a "stress-acceleration" hypothesis and reviewed several examples of neurobehavioral adaptations related to changes in developmental pacing. The foundation for this hypothesis is evidence from animal models indicating that stress-related neurobiology developing in young animals often exhibits more "adult-like" characteristics in response to stressful cues from the environment. For example, early life stress in various forms (e.g., maternal separation/deprivation, premature weaning, insufficient bedding, physical abuse models) has been associated with earlier structural and functional development of the hippocampus, amygdala, and connections between the amygdala and medial prefrontal cortex (mPFC) (Bath et al., 2016; Honeycutt et al., 2020; Moriceau et al., 2009; Ono et al., 2008). Earlier development of these regions is central to emotional learning and produces faster-maturing learning behaviors (e.g., earlier onset of adult-like fear learning, fear extinction, and context conditioning) (Bath et al., 2016; Callaghan & Richardson, 2011). At the same time, these stress-mediated phenotypes induce tradeoffs that increase the risk of later emotion dysregulation (reviewed in Callaghan et al., 2014). Within an evolutionary-developmental framework, these behavioral adaptations may function to accelerate independence (e.g., earlier assessment of and reckoning within unsafe environments). Such adaptations may confer survival advantages in harsh, unpredictable early environments, but have longer-term costs (e.g., truncated developmental plasticity, internalizing problems) that may manifest when environments change or as the individual ages. Despite these costs, accelerated developmental pacing may eventuate in longer-term changes in biobehavioral systems that are adaptive under harsh conditions (e.g., accelerated reproductive development; Belsky et al., 1991; Ellis, 2004; see also Nettle et al., 2013). A recent meta-analysis of the human literature found that childhood experiences of threat were associated with accelerated biological aging in childhood and adolescence, including more advanced cellular aging and earlier pubertal maturation (Colich et al., 2020).

Paralleling the rodent literature, initial human research suggests that mPFC-limbic circuitry may also exhibit accelerated development following early caregiving-related stress (Bernier et al., 2018; Gee et al., 2013; Lee et al., 2019; Posner et al., 2016; Mareckova et al., 2020; Thijssen et al., 2017, 2020), though evidence for accelerated development of amygdala-mPFC connectivity is mixed (reviewed in McLaughlin et al., 2019). In a community-based study in Singapore, insensitive caregiving correlated with both larger hippocampal volume in infants (Rifkin-Graboi et al., 2015) and better performance on a hippocampus-based relational memory task (Rifkin-Graboi et al., 2018). Further, postnatal maternal anxiety was positively associated with hippocampal growth from birth to six months of age (Qiu et al., 2013). To our knowledge, this is the first study to test for potentially stress-adapted skills in relation to accelerated development of emotion-related neurobiology. Although the animal literature has provided strong support for the stress acceleration hypothesis, much more longitudinal evidence is needed to confidently support this hypothesis in humans.

3.3 Conclusion

In total, research on early brain development in the context of adversity is consistent with the idea of developmental adaptation to stress in the form of hidden talents (e.g., faster-maturing learning behaviors, better goal-directed behavior in ecologically relevant contexts, stress-adapted decision-making strategies) and other related phenotypes (e.g., disinhibited social engagement, heightened anxiety, threat sensitivity). Although changes in neurobehavioral phenotypes following early adversity involve tradeoffs, with some costs to function (e.g., lower cognitive control, increased morbidity and mortality risk later in life), these changes appear to be adaptively calibrated to harsh, unpredictable environments. To better understand such tradeoffs – and their implications – extant datasets and published neurobehavioral findings on early life stress highlighting deficits could be reexamined to consider whether impairments in one domain are offset by enhancements in another. In turn, new studies could incorporate appropriate measures to specifically test for the neural bases of hidden talents and their development. Both of these approaches could help move the field toward a more balanced understanding of neurobehavioral adaptations to early adversity.

4 Hidden Talents as Adaptive Intelligence

Theory and research in neural plasticity, human intelligence, and evolutionary biology share an explanatory focus on how individuals adapt to their environments. A widely held assumption in evolutionary biology is that, in most species, single "best" strategies for survival and reproduction are unlikely to evolve. This is because the best strategy varies as a function of the physical, economic, and social parameters of one's environment, and thus a strategy that promotes success in some environmental contexts may lead to failure in others (Ellis & Del Giudice, 2019). Selection pressures therefore tend to favor *adaptive phenotypic plasticity*, the capacity of a single genotype to support a range of phenotypes that promote survival and reproduction under different ecological conditions. We have hypothesized that hidden talents – the development of an adaptive suite of physical, social, and cognitive skills that are specialized for harsh, unpredictable environments – represent the outcome of adaptive phenotypic plasticity (Ellis et al., 2017; Frankenhuis & de Weerth, 2013).

Although individual differences in personality are influenced by genetically mediated biological structures and processes (e.g., McCrae & Costa, 1997), personality-relevant traits – including specific physical, social, and cognitive skills – are also shaped by the different social and ecological niches that people inhabit (Durkee et al., 2022; Smaldino et al., 2019). Because different traits afford different payoffs in different niches, people tend to calibrate their traits to the opportunities and constraints afforded by their lived environments (Durkee et al., 2022; Smaldino et al., 2019). This includes calibration of skills and abilities to local conditions. For example, in the twentieth century, adaptation to increasing academic, technological, and other demands of modern society contributed to large increases in conventional intelligence test scores (Flynn, 2016; Giangrande et al., 2022).

Tailoring skills and abilities to the demands of local environments is an important aspect of intelligence. Indeed, intelligence is typically defined at least in part as "adaptation to the environment" (i.e., *adaptive intelligence*; Sternberg, 2019, 2021a). We propose that developmental adaptation to harsh, unpredictable environments shapes adaptive intelligence by presenting the individual with daunting challenges and problems to solve; hidden talents develop as adaptive solutions to such problems and challenges. But are hidden talents "intelligence"? Obviously it depends on one's definition. If one defines intelligence as general cognitive or problem-solving ability – independent of the problems' history or current context – then the answer generally may be "no." But if one defines intelligence as adaptation to the environment as it varies over space and time (Greenfield, 2020; Sternberg, 2017), the answer almost certainly is "yes." *Adaptive intelligence can be understood as one's ability to accomplish tasks that reflect significant challenges within the constraints posed by one's lived environment* (as well as related environments, current or future, that share basic parameters). Much of adaptive intelligence is tacit insofar as it is gained through everyday experience without being openly expressed or explicitly stated (Sternberg & Hedlund, 2002).

4.1 Development of Executive Function Supports Adaptive Intelligence

Consistent with the concept of adaptive intelligence, Doebel (2020) describes how executive function developmentally adapts to lived experiences, and especially to specific tasks in one's environment. Cognitive scientists have traditionally viewed the development of executive function as driven by a set of endogenous neurocognitive mechanisms (e.g., inhibition, increased capacity for reflection, maintenance of abstract representations in working memory). A widely held assumption is that these neurocognitive mechanisms are subserved by prefrontal cortical development and underlie self-regulatory and complex goal-directed behaviors across a range of situations (Doebel, 2020). Likewise, much of the literature on abilities and talents has viewed such characteristics, metaphorically, as residing within the person. By this view, abilities and talents are trait-like, and the purpose of tests is to draw them out and measure them. Accordingly, intelligence has historically been seen as a relatively fixed trait that is general (*g*) and applies across different tasks or challenges, regardless of context (e.g., Deary et al., 2009; Gottfredson, 1997; Sackett et al., 2020).

An alternative set of assumptions is that abilities do not so much inhere within the person as represent a person x task x situation interaction (Sternberg, 2021b). In line with this idea, Doebel (2020) has challenged traditional neuro-developmental accounts of executive function, arguing that they "do not adequately take into account that executive function is always used in relation to specific goals that affect how it is used and develops" (p. 950). Most critically, executive-function skills are contextually contingent (see Section 2); they depend on knowledge, beliefs, norms, values, and preferences, which are activated by and influence the specific goal at hand (Doebel, 2020). For example, seeing adults behave in an unreliable or untrustworthy manner reduces children's willingness to delay gratification (Kidd et al., 2013; Michaelson & Munakata, 2016; Moffett et al., 2020). Such context dependency is why, Doebel argues, standard laboratory measures of executive function do not consistently correlate with questionnaire measures of self-regulation or with many real-world outcomes of interest.

Context-dependence links executive functions to adaptive intelligence. As defined here, adaptive intelligence does not primarily concern performance on standard executive function tasks under decontextualized conditions; that is not adaptation to the environment. Rather, adaptive intelligence concerns the ability to accomplish meaningful tasks in one's lived environment. Adaptive intelligence thus provides a framework for Doebel's (2020) conceptualization of executive function as reflecting the child's ability to exert control in the service of specific, contextually relevant goals (such as using contextual cues to appropriately calibrate delay of gratification or attention shifting) vis-à-vis the child's knowledge, beliefs, values, etc. Further, how people adapt executive-function skills to context may depend on childhood experiences, such as growing up in an unpredictable home environment (Mittal et al., 2015; Young et al., 2018).

4.2 Hidden Talents as Adaptive Intelligence in Relation to the Niche of Childhood Adversity

Applications of the concept of adaptive intelligence necessarily involve describing the lived environment (i.e., the parameters of the experienced environment that a person adapts to). From a hidden talents perspective – focusing on developmental adaptation to stress – the relevant lived environment is the niche of childhood adversity. This niche can be conceptualized in terms of adaptive problems (Ellis, Sheridan et al., 2022). From an evolutionary-developmental perspective, the defining adaptive problem faced by children in contexts of adversity is extrinsic morbidity–mortality, or *harshness*, which refers to external sources of disability and death (Ellis et al., 2009; Quinlan, 2007). As noted earlier (Section 1.1), harshness constitutes at least two distinct adaptive problems: morbidity–mortality from harm imposed by other agents (i.e., threat-based forms of harshness) and morbidity–mortality from insufficient environmental inputs (i.e., deprivation-based forms of harshness) (Ellis, Sheridan et al., 2022). Threat-based forms of harshness encompass experiences involving actual harm or threat of harm to the child's survival, including direct victimization experiences (e.g., physical abuse, sexual abuse), those witnessed by the child (e.g., violence between caregivers), and ecological factors related to threat (e.g., warfare, neighborhood violence). Deprivation-based forms of harshness, in contrast, involve limited or reduced material, energetic, or social/cognitive inputs from the environment during development (e.g., neglect, inadequate access to food, the absence of a primary caregiver, low levels of cognitive stimulation), as well as ecological factors related to deprivation (e.g., poverty, destruction of food supplies by pestilence or weather). Both experiences of threat and deprivation can vary stochastically, making unpredictability along both of these dimensions another adaptive problem faced by children growing up in contexts of adversity (Ellis, Sheridan et al., 2022; see Young et al., 2020, for a discussion of different types of unpredictability, which may pose different adaptive problems). For example, economic deprivation tends to strain relationships between parents; thus, children raised in poverty experience relatively high levels of parental relationship disruption (e.g., Watson & McLanahan, 2011), creating a link between economic deprivation and family unpredictability. Taken together, threat, deprivation, and unpredictability are developmental contexts that children inhabit in lasting and pervasive ways, such as through elevated family violence, less safe neighborhoods, parental job instability, caregiver transitions, chaotic home environments, less parental scaffolding of child learning, limited housing options, food insecurity, homelessness, social marginalization (e.g., racism), and low rank vis-à-vis others in the social class hierarchy. These related contexts shape the social/ecological niche of childhood adversity.

Hidden talents can be understood as a form of adaptive intelligence, reflecting particular skills related to solving adaptive problems encountered when growing up in the niche of childhood adversity. Further, experiences in this niche may functionally alter development in ways that promote adaptation to anticipated future environments (such as using experiences of childhood unpredictability as a basis for altering cognitive development in ways that upregulate attention shifting or working-memory updating; see Section 2).

Consistent with Doebel's (2020) model of executive-function development, mental contents such as knowledge, beliefs, and values acquired through development in the niche of childhood adversity may reflect, activate, and guide hidden talents. Knowledge includes socially/ecologically relevant information, such as knowing how to deal with dangerous situations, awareness of surrounding stimuli in one's perceptual field (Grossman & Varnum, 2011), and understanding self and others' position in social hierarchies (Frankenhuis, de Vries et al., 2020). Beliefs include socially/ecologically relevant inferences or biases, such as the tendency to attribute social causality to the situation rather than the individual (Grossman & Varnum, 2011; Kraus et al., 2009), perceptions that other people cannot be trusted or future outcomes cannot be predicted or controlled (Cabeza de Baca et al., 2016; Ross & Hill, 2002), and inferences regarding the likelihood of dying at a young age (e.g., Chisholm et al., 2005; Dickerson & Quas, 2021). Values may by instantiated in socially/ecologically relevant priorities, such as a preference for more immediate over delayed rewards (Daly & Wilson, 2005; Pepper & Nettle, 2017), a focus on current threats and opportunities (Frankenhuis et al., 2016), and a preference for concreteness in learning and practical applications of knowledge relevant to one's lived experiences (VanTassel-Baska, 2018). These socially and ecologically based cognitions – knowledge, beliefs, values – may be critical to understanding how children develop and apply hidden talents to solve relevant adaptive problems encountered in the niche of childhood adversity.

4.3 Hidden Talents as Cultural Capital

Hidden talents can also be understood as a form of *cultural capital*: the accumulation of specific forms of knowledge, skills and abilities among particular social or cultural groups (Yosso, 2005). Ogbu (1981) describes cultural capital in terms of instrumental competencies that functionally develop – through child rearing and adolescent socialization processes that reflect the environmental demands faced by a given group – in relation to cultural-ecological contexts. This tailoring of instrumental competencies to lived experiences is a form of adaptive intelligence. Indeed, experience-based knowledge relevant to solving practical problems in a given domain (e.g., folk medicine, hunting, social-dominance relationships) is particularly important to adaptive intelligence (and may be distinctive from what is captured by IQ tests). For example, rural Kenyan children who had more adaptive procedural knowledge (for self-medicating with natural herbal medicines used to combat parasitic illnesses) actually had less academic declarative and procedural knowledge, as shown by slightly lower IQ scores and school achievement (Sternberg et al., 2001). Likewise, in a study of Native American Yup'ik people in Alaska, rural adolescents surpassed urban adolescents in tests of practical adaptive intelligence (with items covering everyday-life knowledge of topics such as hunting, gathering, and location-finding), whereas the urban adolescents performed better on conventional measures of fluid and crystallized intelligence (Grigorenko et al., 2004). Such conventional intelligence tests were presumably better matched to significant challenges and opportunities faced in more urban environments (involving more abstract, analytical problem-solving). The measure of practical adaptive intelligence predicted acquisition of Yup'ik-valued practical skills (as rated by adult community members) in ways that were complementary to, and in some cases incremental to, the prediction provided by the conventional intelligence test scores.

The concept of adaptive intelligence is also relevant to understanding skill sets in children growing up in collectivist societies. In that context, children are accustomed to confronting problems in groups rather than individually. Dominant Western values are not collectivist. Within our individualist culture, people from many nondominant collectivist communities, such as children from a number of Indigenous-heritage communities of the Americas, are often viewed from a deficit perspective because they do not perform well in mainstream, middle-class institutions such as schools (Rogoff et al., 2017). Consistent with the idea of hidden talents, however, such children display enhanced skills that are relevant in their social/ecological niche. These skills include enhanced collaborative abilities (e.g., working together in particularly fluid and skilled coordination) and attentiveness to surrounding events (e.g., skillfully and simultaneously attending to multiple events that do not directly involve the child) relative to peers who have had greater exposure to Western mass schooling (reviewed in Rogoff et al., 2017). Although such skills are not appropriately construed as stress-adapted, this research on children in collectivist societies provides another example of cultural capital as adaptive intelligence. Children in these societies bring socially/ecologically relevant skills to the table, even if those skills are not adequately recognized or valued in Western models of education and achievement.

In discussing the cross-cultural literature on hidden talents as adaptive intelligence/cultural capital, the point is not to downplay the importance of succeeding in mainstream contexts such as school or formal employment; that is of course of the utmost importance. Success in mainstream contexts, however, does not conflict with – and could be enhanced by – approaches that identify, value, and leverage hidden talents (see Sections 5 and 6). Likewise, the current focus on hidden talents does not imply that intelligence as measured by IQ tests lacks value, or is not relevant to adaptation. Rather, the point is that measurement of IQ is partly through tests of acculturation and socialization that reflect the experiences of children who are primarily middle-class and growing up in a "modernized" society (Flynn & Sternberg, 2020; Richardson, 2002). Indeed, a recent meta-analysis of 142 effect sizes across 42 data sets involving over 600,000 participants found that formal education itself boosts IQ scores (Ritchie & Tucker-Drob, 2018), as do programs that directly target academic skill instruction (e.g., reading, math, language), as shown in another meta-analysis (Stockard et al., 2018).

In many low- and middle-income countries, children grow up with more survival-challenging experiences. They may see far less of Western-style schooling (the kind that promotes abstract, analytical thinking), or be given fewer opportunities to learn from it, thereby disadvantaging them on IQ tests. As in the Kenyan, Yup'ik, and collectivist examples, young people may instead display their intelligence in more practical ways, often leveraging their cultural capital in ways that are adaptive in context. In many cases, this includes development of stress-adapted skills and knowledge that enable people to accomplish tasks that reflect significant challenges within the constraints of harsh, unpredictable environments. In India, for example, limited access to resources and infrastructure is thought to promote a form of creative improvisation known as *jugaad* (the ability to achieve frugal or makeshift solutions by using resources at hand in novel ways, such as cobbling together local materials to build a truck; e.g., Singh et al., 2012). The myriad capabilities of street youth, including potentially heightened creativity (Dahlman et al., 2013), are consistent with this idea (see Bender et al., 2007; Malindi & Theron, 2010; Panter-Brick, 2002). A similar logic applies to individuals from lower-SES backgrounds in Western societies, who tend to score lower on IQ tests than their higher-SES peers (e.g., Heberle & Carter, 2015; von Stumm & Plomin, 2015), but may display adaptive intelligence in relation to challenges faced in their local environments (as reviewed in Section 2). To more clearly discriminate between adaptive intelligence and general intelligence, future research should test whether measures of hidden talents are *g*-loaded within adversity-exposed populations. When using ecologically relevant measures of hidden talents (see Young et al., 2022), we expect that hidden talents will not load heavily on *g*, as per the following case study of the Tsimané.

4.4 The Tsimané: A Case Study of Schooling, Cognitive Performance, and Adaptive Intelligence

Many of the foregoing principles regarding adaptive intelligence have been demonstrated in a body of research on the Tsimané, an Indigenous group of forager-horticulturalists living in the Bolivian Amazon. This research has focused on both ecologically relevant skills and abstract reasoning/problem-solving abilities. The Tsimané inhabit a harsh social/ecological niche characterized by high childhood mortality, relatively short life expectancy, high rates of injury and illness, food shortages, kin and partner death, social conflict, and marginalization and encroachment by colonizing Bolivian nationals (Gurven et al., 2007, 2015). Facing these challenges presents myriad adaptive problems to the Tsimané; solutions to these problems require complex socially and ecologically relevant skills. One such capacity, well-documented among the Tsimané, is the ability to spatially navigate long distances through dense vegetation to find food, search for mates, visit other communities, and the like, while avoiding predators and other threats (e.g., Davis, Stack et al., 2021). Although the fitness correlates of spatial navigation have not been studied among the Tsimané, research with Twa forager-pastoralists in Namibia has linked variation between males in spatial ability and range size to indicators of reproductive success (Vashro & Cashdan, 2015). Another important skill set among the Tsimané involves ethnobotanical knowledge, such as the ability to identify useful plants and accurately use them. Among the Tsimané, ethnobotanical skills are associated with positive life outcomes and economic returns, such as improved nutritional status, child health, and crop diversity (reviewed in Reyes-García et al., 2010). In total, complex skills, such as spatial-navigational ability and ethnobotanical knowledge, exemplify adaptive intelligence, enabling individuals to accomplish challenging tasks related to survival and reproduction within the constraints of the Tsimané's lived environment.

Education reforms implemented in Bolivia in the mid-2000s resulted in wide variation in the availability and quality of schooling across Tsimané communities (though at low levels of schooling overall). This variation occurred across Tsimané villages belonging to the same ethnolinguistic group and inhabiting a relatively uniform cultural/ecological niche without significant material wealth or wealth inequality (Davis, 2014; Davis, Stieglitz et al., 2021). This heterogeneity in schooling across otherwise homogenous communities afforded an opportunity to examine the differential effects of schooling on cognitive performance. In a cross-sectional analysis of Tsimané people across the life course, Gurven et al. (2017) found that measures of fluid intelligence and processing speed (e.g., verbal declarative memory, attention, psychomotor speed) were positively associated with formal schooling in all age groups; that substantial school-based advantages were already present at the earliest age of assessment (age eight); and that these effects were greater in villages with more experienced teachers and higher-quality schools. Extending this work, Davis, Stieglitz et al. (2021), in a four-year longitudinal analysis of Tsimané children aged eight to eighteen, found that children in high-quality schools showed a mean 47 percent *increase*, but that children in low-quality schools showed a mean 2 percent *decrease*, in abstract reasoning ability (assessed by Raven's Colored Progressive Matrices) over the time period of the study. In total, the Tsimané data provide strong support for the hypothesis that formal schooling enhances abstract, analytical reasoning. Such reasoning abilities – reflecting fluid intelligence – can presumably be applied across domains in ways that support problem-solving in novel situations.

Yet fluid intelligence is not equivalent to adaptive intelligence. Abstract reasoning abilities may have limited utility for accomplishing tasks that reflect significant challenges within the constraints imposed by the Tsimané's lived environment, as evidenced by tradeoffs between formal schooling and ecologically relevant skills. In general, people who have not been exposed to formal schooling find reasoning about abstract categories to be highly counterintuitive (Cole & Means, 1981; Davis, Stieglitz et al., 2021; Luria, 1976). Among Tsimané children, a composite measure of performance on cognitive tasks requiring abstraction without ecological context (e.g., Raven's Colored Progressive Matrices) – a measure that the researchers used as a proxy for school exposure – was negatively correlated with navigational ability (as indicated by accuracy on a dead reckoning task), possibly due to time allocation tradeoffs between schooling and wayfaring (Davis & Cashdan, 2019). Among Tsimané adults, measures of schooling and school-related abilities (i.e., math, reading, writing) were negatively associated with ethnobotanical knowledge (Reyes-García et al., 2010). Likewise, Tsimané raised in more urban areas or nontraditional villages, who have relatively high exposure to schooling, rarely achieve a high level of hunting proficiency (Gurven et al., 2006). In total, increases in abstract, analytical skills associated with schooling do not apparently translate into adaptive intelligence – as used in daily life in a contextualized way – vis-à-vis the Tsimané's native ecology (even if such skills help Tsimané people integrate into Bolivia's market-based economy). These Tsimané data converge with a larger literature demonstrating relatively weak associations between scores on traditional intelligence tests and skill at solving social and practical problems encountered in everyday life (Richardson, 2002; Sternberg, 1999, 2002; cf. Gottfredson, 2003, for an opposing viewpoint).

4.5 Conclusion

Differences in conceptions of intelligence around the world are common (Sternberg, 2017). A conception of intelligence in rural Kenya, for example, involves elements of creative, practical, and wise thinking (Grigorenko et al., 2001), which differs from viewing intelligence as being able to think and reason abstractly or solve problems in novel situations. Indigenous conceptions of intelligence, in general, tend to be much more practically oriented, often reflecting the ability to engage and cope with typically stressful challenges posed by local environments (Greenfield, 1997; Sternberg, 2017), such as those faced by the Yup'ik or Tsimané. In this section, we have conceptualized hidden talents as a form of adaptive intelligence (as opposed to general intelligence). This converges with a core assumption of the hidden talents model: that hidden talents, as used in daily life in a contextualized way, reflect particular skills and forms of knowledge that enable one to function (e.g., survive, obtain resources, navigate significant challenges) within the constraints imposed by harsh, unpredictable environments. Adapting to such environments promotes the development – and situational expression (e.g., sensitization effects) – of stress-adapted skills in the service of contextually relevant goals.

We have proposed that hidden talents can be understood as solutions to adaptive problems posed by the niche of childhood adversity. In many cases, these solutions are instantiated in cultural capital. Indeed, as shown in a large cultural literature, many instrumental competencies develop in response to environmental demands faced by particular social or cultural groups and play an integral role in adapting to the environment. Advanced navigational skills, ethnobotanical knowledge, and collaborative abilities are a few examples discussed in this section. This extends hidden talents into a cultural realm beyond what is typically studied in Westernized contexts. Although research on cultural capital is potentially well-positioned to uncover stress-adapted skills, it must be appreciated that cultural capital is a broader construct than hidden talents. The latter is specific to adversity. Development of hidden talents is thus conceptually distinct from more general processes involved in the acquisition of locally relevant skills and knowledge, which may occur independently of developmental adaptations to stress (see further discussion in Section 5).

This conceptualization of hidden talents as adaptive intelligence informs measurement of stress-adapted skills. The hidden talents approach seeks to capture the abilities of stress-adapted people using test settings and materials that are ecologically relevant to their lives (Young et al., 2022), as conventional instruments and assessment methods may not be suited to measuring stress-adapted skills. For instance, standard cognitive tasks typically require prolonged sustained attention (e.g., Raven's Progressive Matrices), which is likely to disadvantage people who have adapted to unpredictable conditions (see Mittal et al., 2015). Although a large literature has linked formal schooling to better performance on abstract cognitive tests (e.g., Ceci, 1991; Ritchie & Tucker-Drob, 2018; Stockard et al., 2018), as per the Tsimané case study, this literature is based on cognitive tests that employ *two-dimensional stimuli* (e.g., line drawings, photographs, patterns), often presented on computer screens. However, in a cross-cultural study that used familiar *three-dimensional stimuli* (i.e., beads and cubes), no relations emerged between formal education and either visuospatial working memory or short-term memory, despite wide variation in years of schooling across diverse populations in low- and middle-income countries (Dutra et al., 2022). This finding converges with the literature reviewed earlier on the importance of assessing hidden talents in ways that are ecologically relevant to adversity-exposed children (see Section 2).

If growing up in harsh environments fosters adaptive intelligence in the form of hidden talents, then it becomes important to consider how these talents can be harnessed to promote success in other (mainstream) contexts, including institutional settings that prepare young people for success in work and civic life. One possibility, for example, is that teaching and learning strategies that use ecologically relevant three-dimensional stimuli (e.g., materials from children's everyday environments), rather than abstract two-dimensional stimuli, could help to uncover and actualize stress-adapted skills. Building on this logic, we next consider how leveraging hidden talents in stress-adapted children and youth could provide important pathways to success in school.

5 Leveraging Hidden Talents in Education

The hidden talents approach conceptualizes children and youth who are stress-adapted as socially and cognitively skilled at functioning in harsh, unpredictable environments. Instead of recognizing these capabilities, however, and utilizing them as building blocks for success, stress-adapted skills are rarely measured or understood in school systems. That is a lost opportunity in our view, and the goal of this section is to begin filling in this gap.

The evidence linking low income and economic marginalization to lower educational achievement in children is incontrovertible (e.g., Duncan et al., 2017). For example, in member countries of the Organization for Economic Co-operation and Development, results from the Program for International Student Assessment (PISA) – focusing on reading, mathematics, and science literacy in 15-year-olds – show a gap of 0.7 to 0.8 standard deviations between students in the bottom versus the top 15 percent of the PISA index of economic, social, and cultural status (Dietrichson et al., 2017).

Various intervention strategies have been developed to address these disparities. One approach focuses on mitigating risk (i.e., changing the environment), such as through poverty-reduction programs (e.g., Duncan et al., 2017), or by increasing cognitive stimulation or providing other environmental enrichments for children experiencing poverty (e.g., Obradović et al., 2016; Romeo et al., 2021; Yousafzai et al., 2016). Another approach focuses on ameliorating deficits (i.e., changing the person), such as through programs designed to boost executive function or other neurocognitive skills (e.g., Blair & Raver, 2014; Distefano et al., 2020; Zelazo, 2020), or through targeted school-based interventions for improving academic achievement (e.g., tutoring, after-school programs; reviewed in Dietrichson et al., 2017). This approach also includes social psychological interventions, which attempt to reduce educational disparities by changing individual learners' perspectives or ways of making meaning (e.g., growth mindset interventions, utility-value interventions, social-belonging interventions; reviewed in Brady et al., 2017). Complementing these approaches are programs designed to foster appropriate classroom behavior in underserved students (e.g., SLANT: Sit up, Listen, Ask and answers questions, Nod your head, and Track the speaker; see Calarco, 2018).

Meta-analyses have shown that school-based academic interventions can meaningfully improve the academic performance of socioeconomically disadvantaged students (with small to moderate effect sizes depending on the type of program; Dietrichson et al., 2017); however, such interventions do not come close to closing the achievement gap.[5] Further, positive effects at the end of an intervention do not necessarily translate into positive effects over time. In the only randomized control study of a statewide prekindergarten program serving low-income families, initial positive effects on academic achievement measures (e.g., literacy, mathematics) at the end of preschool faded out by the end of kindergarten and became iatrogenic by the end of the third grade, with negative effects on both achievement and

---

[5] The achievement gap refers specifically to disparities in performance according to standard metrics of school success (e.g., grade point average, standardized test scores, graduation rates). Disparities in academic achievement do not imply disparities in the capacity to solve problems or accomplish tasks in relation to the challenges posed by one's lived environment (see Section 4). The achievement gap more narrowly reflects differences in what counts as knowing and being successful in school according to normative, middle class standards. Social justice frameworks in education contend that the achievement gap arises from disparities in the educational opportunities and supports available to marginalized/minoritized students relative to their White and Asian peers (e.g., Goldenberg, 2014). The hidden talents approach assumes that different environmental conditions promote the development of different kinds of skills. Thus, to a significant extent, the achievement gap may reflect different *kinds* of achievement/skills (as opposed to different *levels* of achievement/skills), as reviewed in Section 2.

behavioral problems increasing in magnitude by the sixth grade (Durkin et al., 2022; Pion & Lipsey, 2021).

In total, traditional approaches to intervention, such as prekindergarten programs, use a variety of strategies to support the development of skills needed to succeed in school. These approaches support children growing up under harsh/unpredictable conditions to have environmental experiences (i.e., mitigate risk) and/or to think and act (i.e., ameliorate deficits) in ways more typical of children growing up under safe/supportive/stable conditions. Although mitigating risk and ameliorating deficits are relevant strategies, we argue that they represent only part of the solution. Leveraging hidden talents is another potential strategy, shifting the emphasis toward adaptive intelligence.

The application of the hidden talents model to educational practice builds on a central tenet of learning theory: that individuals acquire new information more readily when prior knowledge and abilities serve as the foundation for learning (Committee on Developments in the Science of Learning, 1999). In current school contexts, however, standard curriculum and instructional practices are often mismatched to the prior knowledge and abilities of stress-adapted students. This mismatch is potentially far-reaching; it includes not only what social and cognitive skills are valued in the classroom, but also language usage, cognitive tendencies, self-presentation, behavioral norms and expectations, and personal and interpersonal functioning (e.g., Ellis et al., 2017; Gallimore & Goldenberg, 2001; Hoff, 2013; Stephens et al., 2019; Richardson et al., 2016).

Such mismatch may be expressed as apparent shortcomings in stress-adapted students, as in the case of certain academic skills (e.g., using a big vocabulary, decoding printed words, being able to quickly process large numbers or abstract geometric shapes), or in terms of abstract, analytical reasoning (e.g., the ability to maintain abstract representations in working memory, the willingness to focus on a few abstract details of a problem rather than its larger context; see Section 4). Conversely, mismatch may arise from the specific qualities that stress-adapted students bring to the table, such as the need for more immediate over delayed rewards, reticence to engage in self-advocacy in classroom contexts, heightened attention shifting, and/or the calibration of learning mechanisms to elevated levels of threat, chaos, or uncertainty (Ellis, Sheridan et al., 2022; Pepper & Nettle, 2017; Stephens et al., 2019; see also Section 2). Traditional approaches to intervention view these characteristics of stress-adapted students as problems to be remedied. From this perspective, addressing the mismatch between home and school environments often involves the Sisyphean task of changing stress-adapted skills and habits (see Calarco, 2018; Ellis et al., 2017).

Intervening to change developmental adaptations to stress, however, is not the only way forward. Working with, rather than against, hidden talents in educational contexts affords an alternative pathway to fostering school success in stress-adapted students. This pathway aligns with the broader movement in educational theory and research away from deficit perspectives toward approaches that build on the values, behavior, and cultural capital of diverse children and families (see Fikrat-Wevers et al., 2021). The hidden talents approach does not stigmatize students who have grown up under challenging conditions; rather, it recognizes stress-adapted students for their skills. Here we suggest ways to incorporate and engage hidden talents in teaching and learning strategies. We both highlight existing pedagogy that is consistent with a hidden talents approach and suggest novel teaching and learning strategies inspired by this approach. Our goal is to guide future research and practice by describing the contours of the hidden talents approach to education, rather than to articulate fully developed strategies that are ready to implement in the classroom. (The necessary steps needed to incorporate a hidden talents approach into the classroom are discussed in Sections 5.4 and 5.5.)

5.1 Implementing Instructional Strategies That Leverage Hidden Talents

The most straightforward application of the hidden talents approach is to employ instructional strategies that capitalize on stress-adapted skills. Many children raised in poverty do not have a quiet room where they can work undisturbed on school assignments. They may instead need to efficiently *shift their attention* back and forth between their homework and other pressing family and environmental demands while *tracking changing information* (see Blair & Raver, 2012; Evans et al., 2005, which show that children from low-SES homes experience elevated levels of crowding, noise, volatility, and unpredictability in their lives). Adapting to such challenging contexts may foster the development of particular skills, which could be harnessed to maximize performance of stress-adapted children and youth.

For example, if stress-adapted people tend to display less sustained attention (e.g., weaker focus on a particular target in the environment, less filtering of distractor stimuli) but are adept at shifting their attention between different tasks (Fields et al., 2021; Mittal et al., 2015; Pope et al., 2019; though see Nweze et al., 2021), then redesigning instructional practices to leverage attention shifting skills could potentiate their learning. This translates into rethinking standard approaches (e.g., focusing on completing single school assignments in a quiet room, displaying content in static print) relative to alternative approaches (e.g., studying in a room with more background noise, regularly changing focus and switching between assignments, displaying content on dynamic touch screens). It remains an open empirical question, however, which of these adjustments improve learning. For instance, it is possible that studying in a room with more background noise actually impedes learning in stress-adapted youth, but that displaying content on dynamic touch screens improves it. If so, that would be an important discovery.

Likewise, if stress-adapted students tend to have lower working-memory capacity but are especially good at tracking information in their environment and replacing older information that is no longer relevant with new, updated information (Young et al., 2018), this enhanced working-memory updating ability could lead them to excel when learning in information-rich environments that are frequently changing. This may be particularly true when the changing information involves ecologically relevant stimuli (Young et al., 2022). This again translates into rethinking standard approaches (e.g., learning through rote memorization, retaining information even when it is not situationally relevant, providing feedback days after completing an assignment) relative to alternative approaches (e.g., creating learning environments that are more fluid and allow students to apply skills in changing contexts; providing students with real-time feedback regarding performance on tasks, so as to leverage their efficient working-memory updating capacity to replace incorrect strategies and responses with correct ones).

At the same time, the success of these strategies may depend on classroom environments. People from more stressful, chaotic backgrounds appear to elevate their performance on attention shifting and working-memory updating tasks in contexts that make salient the reality of daily stressors and uncertainties (Mittal et al., 2015; Young et al., 2018). This context-dependent performance converges with research showing that assessment of executive functions in a naturalistic classroom setting better predicts later academic achievement than does assessment in more controlled, conventional one-on-one settings (Obradović et al., 2018). Other research, investigating culturally responsive teaching methods, has more broadly demonstrated the effects of classroom context on learning, particularly in students of color. This work has documented a variety of ways to structure classroom environments to improve the academic performance of ethnically and racially diverse students (e.g., multicultural curriculum content, use of motion and movement, music, frequent variability in tasks and formats, dramatic elements in teaching; reviewed in Gay, 2018). Comparable research is needed to determine how to create more effective classroom environments for stress-adapted students, despite the diversity of their life experiences.

How could these ideas inform instructional practices, such as how to teach Algebra? Conventional teaching methods favor students who have strong working memory capacity and are good at sustaining attention. Such cognitive abilities tend to be enhanced in higher-SES students growing up under stable conditions (Ellis et al., 2017). What if, instead, we taught Algebra in ways that leveraged attention shifting and working-memory updating abilities, potentially under conditions that are closer to the lived environments of stress-adapted students (e.g., not overly quiet or controlled)? That could allow teachers to work with, rather than against, the capacities of stress-adapted students, reducing the *mismatch* between the skills possessed by such students and the skills needed to function well in school. This underscores a critical direction for future research: Testing strategies for effectively leveraging stress-adapted skills and the environmental contexts that facilitate their expression.

One promising line of work builds on research showing that lower-SES students display greater empathic accuracy, compassion, attentiveness to others, and interdependence (Kraus et al., 2012; Piff et al., 2018), which tends to make lower-SES students uncomfortable with the goal of outperforming others in academic contexts (Crouzevialle & Darnon, 2019). This discomfort underscores the importance of motivational context when assessing students who have experienced low-income and economic marginalization. Simply focusing students on the importance of mastery (improving abilities and the quality of learning, increasing and consolidating knowledge) as opposed to performance (distinguishing yourself by performing better than other students) eliminated the performance gap between lower- and higher-SES college students on complex arithmetic problems and exams (Jury et al., 2015; Smeding et al., 2013). Conversely, rendering differences in performance between students visible in the classroom (e.g., by having students raise their hand when they complete a task) substantially increased the performance gap in reading comprehension between lower- and higher-SES sixth graders (Goudeau & Croizet, 2017). This research highlights the importance of focusing instruction on mastery and avoiding (advertently or inadvertently) harmful social comparisons in performance that can magnify socioeconomic disparities.

School curricula and instructional practices could also be structured to capitalize on the interdependence and collaborative abilities of students from lower-SES backgrounds. For example, having college students work collaboratively (where they must work together to achieve a shared goal) versus individually tends to boost the performance of students from working-class backgrounds (Dittmann et al., 2020). In some cases, problem-solving tasks that require students to work together to perform well even confer a performance advantage to working-class students relative to their middle-class peers (Dittmann et al., 2020). Dittmann and colleagues present evidence that this boost in performance results from a specific hidden talent: the tendency of students from working-class backgrounds to engage in more effective group processes. Similarly, meta-analytic reviews have shown that cooperative learning in schoolchildren, especially when it involves interdependent reward contingencies, has positive effects on school achievement, and that these effects are strongest in students who are struggling academically, students from low-income families, and underrepresented minority students (Dietrichson et al., 2017; Pellegrini et al., 2021; Rohrbeck et al., 2003; Slavin et al., 2011). Taken together, this research – spanning primary school, secondary school, and college – underscores the potential benefits of designing curricula and instructional practices to value interdependent teamwork and ensure that students work together on interdependent tasks.

5.2 Anchoring Curriculum in Skills and Concepts That Are Ecologically Relevant in Harsh Environments

Making educational experiences relevant to students – and the role of personal relevance in motivating and energizing student learning – is an area of substantial theory and research (reviewed in Priniski et al., 2018). One approach has been to make connections between what students do in school and their out-of-school lives by customizing academic texts to learners' interests and prior knowledge. In randomized experiments, this form of personalization has meaningfully increased engagement and performance in mathematics among middle and high school students (Bernacki & Walkington, 2018; Clinton & Walkington, 2019; Høgheim & Reber, 2015; Walkington, 2013), particularly when the connections between academic texts and learners' interests/knowledge are relatively deep. Although this research has not specifically examined stress-adapted students, personalization appears to be most effective among students who are struggling with or have low initial interest in math (Høgheim & Reber, 2015; Walkington, 2013).

Personalization varies in granularity, ranging from more general (e.g., instruction is personalized to the members of a particular group) to more specific (e.g., instruction is personalized to a given individual) (Clinton & Walkington, 2019). Anchoring curriculum in skills, topics, and concepts that are ecologically relevant in harsh environments is a form of personalization at the group level. For example, because perceptions of social rank are especially relevant to youth from low-SES backgrounds (Kraus et al., 2012; Piff et al., 2018), such youth may be particularly motivated and able to solve reasoning problems related to social status and dominance. Consider the following logical reasoning problem: Adam is older than Bart, and Bart is older than Chris; who is older, Adam or Chris? The hidden talents approach suggests that stress-adapted students will be better at solving this problem when the content concerns status and rank. For example, Adam is dominant over Bart, and Bart over Chris; who is more dominant, Adam or Chris? Recent research provided partial support for this hypothesis, finding that young adults who had more recent exposure to violence displayed intact or enhanced *memory* for social dominance, but finding no evidence of enhanced *reasoning* about social dominance (Frankenhuis, de Vries et al., 2020). We assume that the relevance of social-dominance content increased levels of interest, and hence attention and motivation, especially for participants who currently live in hostile conditions. These findings on memory for social dominance concur with other memory research suggesting that replacing sterile testing materials with ecologically relevant content from the real world can eliminate, or even reverse, disparities in performance among adversity-exposed children (Rifkin-Graboi et al., 2021; Young et al., 2022).

A research program in the late 1960s tested whether social disparities in performance on scholastic aptitude tests could be reduced through group-level personalization (Carver, 1969; Orr & Graham, 1968). The focal population in this research was low-income Black middle school students in Washington, DC. One aspect of personalization involved content: a sample of male students from the focal population were interviewed about their interests, favorite TV shows, favorite topics of conversation, etc. Another aspect of personalization involved the format through which test items were presented. To avoid confounding with reading ability, test items were spoken rather than written. The vocal patterns of the speaker were personalized to be familiar to the target group and pleasant for them to listen to. To create a Listening Comprehension Test (LCT), stories were recorded in the style of episodes in a radio program, centering on common themes identified in the pretest interviews (e.g., sports, adventure stories, spies). The storyteller then asked multiple-choice questions about the content. The test had good psychometric properties and correlated strongly with standard aptitude tests in both low-income and middle-income Black and White samples. The LCT, along with a standard scholastic aptitude test (the School and College Ability Test; SCAT-II), was then given to a diverse sample of middle schoolers ($N = 615$). There were significant disparities in performance between low-income and middle-income students and between Black and White students on the SCAT-II. However, the gap between low- and middle-income students was substantially reduced on the LCT (from 0.94 standard deviations on the SCAT-II to 0.58 standard deviations on the LCT). This reduction suggests that personalizing the content and format of test questions to match the interests and background of an adversity-exposed group (people with low-income and economic marginalization) can meaningfully reduce disparities in academic performance. Despite this achievement, the LCT was ultimately abandoned because it was not similarly successful in reducing disparities between Black and White students.

5.2.1 Strengths-Based, Culturally Responsive Approaches to Leveraging Ecocultural Assets in Diverse Children Experiencing Marginalization

Fast-forwarding to the present, a current strength-based approach involves personalizing the content of educational interventions to better serve communities of color. Indeed, as we move toward uncovering a high-resolution map of hidden talents, there should be many opportunities to anchor instruction and curricula in the ecologically relevant skills and ecocultural assets that diverse children bring to the table. This idea has already been implemented in some culturally responsive interventions designed to work with the skills, interests, and background of diverse children living in poverty and experiencing marginalization (for reviews, see Brady et al., 2017; Gay, 2018; Perez-Brena et al., 2018). Here we discuss two examples: *ethnomathematics* (teaching math in ways that build on cultural knowledge possessed by students; Furuto, 2014) and *adaptive culture* (cultural values and traditions among minoritized groups that develop in response to social conditions, including marginalization, and play an integral role in adapting to the environment; García Coll et al., 1996; Perez-Brena et al., 2018).

Ethnomathematics has been utilized successfully among rural Yup'ik Alaska Native people. The economic activities of traditional Yup'ik, which involve hunting and gathering over difficult-to-travel tundra in often extreme weather conditions, require many adaptive skills. The Adapting Yup'ik Elders' Knowledge math curriculum uses construction of fish racks (an ecologically relevant skill in rural Yup'ik communities) to teach plane-geometry concepts of area and perimeter (Sternberg et al., 2006). Anchoring instruction in this cultural context increased performance among Yup'ik sixth-graders (relative to other sixth-graders who received conventional textbook-based instruction). The efficacy of teaching math to Yup'ik children based on cultural knowledge has been supported in a randomized controlled trial (Kisker et al., 2012). Most critically, improved understanding of math concepts transferred beyond the cultural context; students in intervention schools performed significantly better than students in control schools on standard math questions that did not make use of any graphics or content contained in the culturally based curriculum.

Other work has focused on harnessing the cultural capital of families experiencing socioeconomic adversity and marginalization. In a randomized trial,

Leyva and colleagues (Leyva, Shapiro et al., 2022; Leyva, Weiland et al., 2022) tested the effects of a strength-based family intervention, which was designed to improve kindergarteners' learning outcomes by leveraging the adaptive culture of Latino families. Most of the parents in the study were immigrants (90 percent) and did not have a high school diploma or equivalent (78 percent). The intervention, Food for Thought (FFT), capitalizes on food routines (e.g., grocery shopping, meal preparation) in the ecocultural context of Latino families. FFT trains parents to embed teaching activities in these routines, such as having children write out a grocery list before going shopping, measure and mix ingredients for cooking, and tell stories about their day during family dinner. FFT had positive effects on child vocabulary and narrative language abilities at the end of the intervention, with suggestive evidence of further impact at a five-month follow up (Leyva, Shapiro et al., 2022; Leyva, Weiland et al., 2022).

In total, both of these culturally responsive interventions were based on understanding and working within the ecocultural niche of a minoritized group. Comparable research is needed to determine how to anchor school and family interventions in skills and concepts that facilitate learning among stress-adapted students. Western educational contexts largely reflect dominant, middle class values, which privilege students who are independent, speak up, express their opinions, question teachers, and pursue their intellectual passions (e.g., Calarco, 2018). Such values may be mismatched to students from lower-income and minoritized backgrounds (Brady et al., 2017). We need to move beyond these dominant values to understand how alternative skill sets and ways of knowing can contribute to being successful in school. That means understanding and working with adaptations to the niche of childhood adversity (even though these adaptations are likely to differ across levels and types of adversity exposures; see Section 1.1).

At the same time, such research would need to be thoughtfully implemented and evaluated, as the use of ecologically relevant stimuli and concepts could potentially undermine performance in some contexts by capturing, distracting, or narrowing attention (e.g., Anderson et al., 2011; Duquennois, 2022). Personalization appears to be most effective when the connections between curriculum/instruction and learners' interests and prior knowledge are relatively deep (Clinton & Walkington, 2019). It may not be enough, therefore, to simply insert words into learning tasks or standardized assessments that relate to students' interests/experiences, or to simply replace abstract stimuli in cognitive tests with real-life stimuli that are more familiar to students. We may instead need to draw on the deeper knowledge students have in relation to actual topics they care about (Clinton & Walkington, 2019), or to embed teaching and learning into everyday activities in the ecocultural context of students' lives (e.g., the FFT intervention, the Adapting Yup'ik Elders' Knowledge math curriculum), or to assess performance in ecologically valid ways related to real-world functioning (e.g., instead of asking children to switch between stimuli presented on a computer screen, they could be asked to switch periodically between practical tasks; Doebel, 2020). These methods could help to anchor teaching, learning, and assessment in skills and concepts that are ecologically relevant to stress-adapted students, potentially increasing their motivation and performance.

5.3 Building on Hidden Talents to Extend Knowledge

Learning in stress-adapted students could be enhanced by using hidden talents as a foundation to extend knowledge, building on skills that stress-adapted students use to solve challenging problems in their lived environments.

5.3.1 Mathematics

Consider child street vendors in Brazil and India, many of whom live in substantial poverty. Research has shown that these children, who perform poorly on abstract math problems, as typically presented in school, do well when asked to perform equally complex computations (such as computing discounts) in the context of market transactions (Banerjee et al., 2017; Carraher et al., 1985). This enhanced math performance in the marketplace was not explained by memorizing combinations of prices and quantities. Furthermore, street vendors were able to generalize their arithmetic skills to correctly carry out market transactions involving other goods they did not sell (Banerjee et al., 2017). The mathematical skills of street vendors provide another example of children developing hidden talents (outside of school), which can transfer (to some extent) to other kinds of nonfamiliar mathematical problems, particularly if pedagogy is designed to leverage these talents.

This approach to teaching mathematics has been implemented successfully in a school-based intervention. Teachers of adversity-exposed (minoritized, low-SES) first-graders were trained to use instructional practices that build on the informal knowledge and invented processes that children already possess for solving addition and subtraction problems (e.g., use of fingers to directly model the action in a word problem; Villaseñor & Kepner, 1993). Students in intervention classrooms, who were taught in ways that leveraged their mathematical thinking, performed much better in solving word problems and completing number facts (50 percent and 73 percent correct, respectively) than did students in control classrooms (11 percent and 15 percent correct, respectively), who received conventional textbook-based instruction. These large effects on mathematics achievement obtained in school districts serving socioeconomically disadvantaged students (Clements et al., 2011; Villaseñor & Kepner, 1993) contrasted with small (though still positive) effects obtained in school districts serving middle-class students (Carpenter et al., 1989). This work converges with theory and research in educational psychology supporting the efficacy of instructional practices that start with concrete materials (i.e., materials that connect with prior knowledge and have referents in students' lived experiences) and then gradually fade to more abstract representations ("concreteness fading"; Fyfe et al., 2014; Fyfe & Nathan, 2019). In total, the work on mathematical thinking underscores the importance – specifically for stress-adapted students – of designing programs of instruction to build on prior knowledge and familiar cognitive processes.

5.3.2 Oral Narrative Skills

Building on hidden talents could also be relevant for improving literacy. If stress-adapted students underperform on standard language assessments (e.g., vocabulary, phonological awareness), but have other highly developed language skills, such as oral narrative fluency and narrative comprehension (e.g., Gardner-Neblett et al., 2012; Miller & Sperry, 2012), these skills could be leveraged to build mastery in language that will promote reading comprehension and related proficiencies.

For example, oral narrative skills appear to be a significant strength in Black children (including those experiencing low-income and economic marginalization), as expressed in vivid, well-developed narratives (e.g., storytelling) that are rich in imagery and have complex organizational structures (Gardner-Neblett et al., 2012; Gardner-Neblett & Iruka, 2015). These oral narrative skills may truly be a hidden talent – one that is not adequately captured by standardized tests of children's oral language abilities. One researcher described conducting a standardized interview to assess language competence in a Black eight-year-old boy. Even though the interviewer was Black, from the neighborhood, and spoke in dialect (African American vernacular), the boy's responses were monosyllabic. That same interviewer later went to the boy's apartment, brought along the boy's best friend, sat on the floor, handed out potato chips, and introduced taboo words and topics (e.g., fighting, peeing). The boy then became an active and fluent participant in the conversation (Labov, 1970). The boy's poor performance on the standardized interview may have resulted from a mismatch between the assessment context (which the boy may have found odd, unsettling, or even threatening; see Kitano, 2010) and how the child used language in his everyday life. In total, the standardized interview was not a social situation that could reveal the child's verbal capabilities.

This general idea was later tested in a study of oral language ability in Black and White five-year-old children from families with low-income and economic marginalization. The children were tested under two counter-balanced conditions: a standard condition (in which open-ended questions were posed in a decontextualized manner) and a thematic condition (in which the same questions were posed in a contextualized manner related to a story plot or an activity that the child was engaged in). In the standard condition, White children outperformed Black children, particularly on more complex and difficult items. This performance gap disappeared, however, in the thematic condition (Fagundes et al., 1998). Although the study was small and needs to be replicated, the improved language performance of Black (but not White) children in the thematic condition may reflect goodness of fit between the contextualized test questions and the conversational patterns that Black children use in daily life in a contextualized way (e.g., in their families and communities). This enhanced performance under more ecologically valid testing conditions converges with our earlier discussion of adaptive intelligence (Section 4).

How can this program of research, showing not only strong oral narrative skills in Black children but also the contexts in which those skills tend to be expressed, be leveraged to support desired educational processes and outcomes? Can educational environments be shaped in ways that promote transfer of these skills toward success in school? The work of Carol Lee affords a promising answer to this question. Lee (1995a) developed a curriculum for teaching literary analysis based on a well-developed oral narrative skill among Black youth: *signifying*. Signifying is a traditional and highly prized form of discourse in Black communities that involves ritualized language play, using innuendo and double meaning in quick verbal repartee, to make fun of someone/ something. Participation in signifying requires complex cognitive abilities, including fast processing of dialogue that is often metaphoric or ironic (Lee, 1995a, 1995b). Lee (1995a) carried out her research in Chicago high schools that served low-income students, were almost entirely Black, and had graduation rates at or below 50 percent. In the intervention classrooms, students read extended signifying dialogues, which they were able to interpret the meaning of relatively easily. The intervention then had students engage in the more challenging task of identifying the strategies they had used to interpret the signifying dialogues, and subsequently to apply those strategies to interpretation of a rich set of literary texts. Students in the experimental classrooms using Lee's curriculum, compared with students in control classrooms who were traditionally taught, demonstrated significantly greater overall gains from pretest to posttest in skill at interpreting fiction, and especially in understanding complex implied relationships (Lee, 1995a; overall gain = 1.5 vs. 0.67 logits in experimental vs. control classrooms).

This research provides an important proof of principle: specific skills displayed by a traditionally marginalized and minoritized group can be leveraged in a school context to promote learning. By intentionally building on a valued social skill – one that had been overlooked in past interventions – this work shows how hidden talents can potentially be used as a foundation to extend knowledge.

5.3.3 Hidden Talents in the Context of Cultural Systems

Consideration of hidden talents as a form of cultural capital is a theme of this Element (see especially Section 4). The work on signifying fits well within this theme. However, many locally relevant skills and forms of knowledge, such as enhanced collaborative abilities among children from some Indigenous-heritage communities of the Americas or knowledge of construction of fish racks among the Yup'ik, are not necessarily stress adapted (i.e., hidden talents). Although general processes involved in the acquisition of locally relevant skills and knowledge are relevant to understanding the development of hidden talents, these processes are conceptually distinct from adaptations to stress (which occur, for example, when developmental exposures to adversity give rise to durable changes in tissues, organs, or brain systems). We have conceptualized hidden talents as solutions to adaptive problems posed by harsh, unpredictable environments. The remarkable survival skills of homeless youth (Bender et al., 2007; Malindi & Theron, 2010; Panter-Brick, 2002) are a case in point. For example, in a Bolivian study comparing boys who were homeless with other equally socioeconomically disadvantaged boys living in houses, the homeless boys scored markedly higher on creativity tests (but not on other cognitive tests) (Dahlman et al., 2013).[6] Heightened creativity in the context of homelessness is presumably a stress-adapted skill for solving problems relevant to surviving on the street – a genuinely harsh and unpredictable environment. This kind of developmental adaptation to stress distinguishes hidden talents from the larger and relatively unconstrained array of specialized skills and forms of knowledge that may arise in the context of any given cultural system. That said, many

---

[6] In a British study, Fry (2018) also compared homeless youth with a comparison group of housed youth on executive functioning and creativity. The comparison group had much lower levels of substance use and contact with the criminal justice system, were much more likely to have completed the necessary secondary qualifications to progress to higher education, and demonstrated better performance on several executive function tasks, especially working memory and impulsivity/risky decision making. Despite these differences, the homeless and housed youth performed comparably on tests of creativity.

adaptations to stress, including development of hidden talents, involve individual as well as social learning and thus are unlikely to occur independent of culture. Relations between hidden talents and cultural systems are a critical area for future theory and research.

5.4 The Kamehameha Early Education Program (KEEP): A Case Study in Leveraging Cultural Capital to Improve Educational Outcomes.

To our knowledge, no existing school curricula or instructional practices have been explicitly designed to leverage the hidden talents of children growing up in harsh environments, particularly at a schoolwide level. The closest approximation we are aware of is the signifying intervention described in Section 5.3.2. One school-based educational program, however, was specifically designed to work with the culturally enhanced (though not necessarily adversity enhanced) capacities of a minoritized group experiencing significant poverty and marginalization. That program, KEEP, provides proof of principle of this strength-based approach in a larger school context. Like the school-based signifying intervention and the family-based FFT intervention (discussed in Section 5.2.1), KEEP leverages cultural capital – harnessing students' ecocultural assets as a vehicle for learning. As opposed to the specific focus of the signifying intervention on literary interpretation, KEEP targeted broader achievement in the language arts.

KEEP was designed for children of native Hawaiian ancestry and culture. Extensive ethnographic research conducted in the late 1960s (reviewed in Jordan, 1984, 1985; Vogt et al., 1987; Weisner et al., 1988) established that native Hawaiian children spent much of their time in children's groups (especially with siblings) and became skilled at teaching and learning from peers. These children's groups were usually mixed in age, shared responsibility for accomplishing important household tasks, and operated largely independently of adult supervision. This independence supported considerable autonomy and self-directed learning in native Hawaiian children. Children's groups were the most common (nonschool) context for acquiring new information and skills, including transmission of culture. As per the Tsimané example discussed earlier (Section 4.4), learning within children's groups, and within the child's natal environment more generally, almost always occurred within an immediately meaningful ecological or family context (supporting development of adaptive intelligence). Overall, these patterns of teaching and learning observed among native Hawaiian children parallel the informal, child-directed educational experiences of children in hunter-gatherer societies (see Gray, 2013) – and thus, in important ways, likely reflect how children evolved to acquire skills and knowledge.

Although native Hawaiian children are successfully socialized into their own culture and acquire many relevant skills and forms of knowledge in that context (Jordan, 1984), these capacities may be mismatched to formal educational contexts (Tharp et al., 2007), as experienced through standard school curricula and instructional practices. This mismatch is manifest in the severe academic underachievement of children of native Hawaiian ancestry and culture (see Jordan, 1984), most of whom grow up in socioeconomically disadvantaged households. This underachievement is reflected in low standardized test scores, high dropout rates, and related behavioral problems (Tharp et al., 2007).

KEEP attempted to reduce this mismatch by remaking school curricula and instructional practices (specifically in language arts) to be more continuous with native Hawaiian culture and ways of learning – leveraging the skills and social interaction patterns of Hawaiian children – with the goal of enhancing educational achievement (Jordan, 1984, 1985; Vogt et al., 1987; Weisner et al., 1988). KEEP transitioned away from whole-class instruction and independent seat-work to small learning groups that facilitated teaching and learning from peers. Building on Hawaiian culture, the learning groups were expected to work cooperatively to complete an assigned learning activity, as well as housekeeping operations in the classroom (e.g., setup, cleanup), without direct supervision by the teacher. Working together in learning groups involved nearly constant verbal and nonverbal exchanges between students. The goal was to harness peer processes for academic purposes (such as by leveraging enhanced skill at assisting others). This approach converges with research discussed earlier (Section 5.1) on the benefits to low-income and minoritized students of having peers work together on interdependent tasks (e.g., Dittmann et al., 2020; Rohrbeck et al., 2003).

Interactions between Hawaiian children and adults tend to be mediated through children's groups; thus, KEEP teachers mostly avoided direct questioning/confrontation with individual students and instead focused on group-addressed questions and volunteered responses, which is a communication pattern that Hawaiian children recognize and respond to. KEEP reading curricula and instructional practices emphasized comprehension – focusing on understanding stories in relation to personal experiences or background knowledge – rather than phonics or mechanics of reading (e.g., decoding sound-symbol relationships). This emphasis on meaning over decontextualized skills worked with, rather than against, the ways in which Hawaiian children acquired skills and information in ecologically relevant contexts at home.

Evaluation of KEEP included (a) case-control studies and (b) a small randomized trial (where first-graders were randomly assigned to either experimental KEEP classrooms or control classrooms that provided instruction as usual)

(Tharp et al., 2007). The case-control studies exclusively involved children from families receiving state public assistance, whereas the randomized trial involved a public school sample that was mostly low-income but more socio-economically diverse. In both the case-control studies and the randomized trial, KEEP students outperformed control students on standardized tests of reading achievement by about one-half standard deviation, with KEEP students performing at a level that approximated national norms (Tharp et al., 2007). It is unclear, however, to what extent these effects maintained over time.

Working on the assumption that diverse students "already possess skills and behaviors that can be utilized in learning what the school has to teach" (Jordan et al., 1992, p. 15), KEEP provides a strong model for development and implementation of curricula and instructional practices that leverage hidden talents. This process begins with research, typically conducted by anthropologists or developmental psychologists, that describes a given cultural or social group, particularly in terms of the environment the group inhabits and their social and cognitive adaptations to that environment (for a good example, see Moll et al., 1992). In the hidden talents research program, that environment is the niche of childhood adversity (as described in Section 4). Applications of theory and research can then serve as a guide – generating ideas for how to incorporate hidden talents into teaching and learning strategies – as articulated in this section. That is a starting point. However, scientists involved in theory and research on hidden talents may not be well prepared to translate education-relevant ideas into educational practice. That would require expertise in instructional design principles, breadth of knowledge regarding acceptable school and classroom practices, practical understanding of what teachers can and cannot readily do in the classroom, and so forth (see Jordan, 1985). Thus, what is needed is close collaboration between researchers studying hidden talents, educational practitioners, and educational researchers in order to choose, shape, and iteratively test curricula and instructional practices that elicit and build on hidden talents in ways that support desired educational processes and outcomes. As per KEEP, this process should be informed by detailed knowledge of sociocultural factors relevant to the target population.

5.5 Further Thoughts on Implementation

Throughout this section we have suggested ways to engage hidden talents in educational contexts. We have both highlighted existing pedagogy that is consistent with a hidden talents approach and suggested novel teaching and learning strategies inspired by this approach. None of our arguments imply, however, that the proposed methods for leveraging hidden talents in education will *only* facilitate learning among adversity-exposed students. Tailoring teaching and learning strategies to stress-adapted students (e.g., orienting instruction and curriculum around real-world thinking and problem-solving) may in some cases benefit all students (e.g., Kisker et al., 2012; also see Section 5.3). When an intervention has positive effects across the board, it can support a universal approach that obviates the need for differentiated instruction – even if the benefits are greater for stress-adapted students, as has been found in many different kinds of universal interventions (Greenberg & Abenavoli, 2017).

At the same time, adapting teaching and learning strategies to stress-adapted students does not always benefit everyone (e.g., Dittmann et al., 2020; Fagundes et al., 1998). Stated differently, there are contexts in which it is best to personalize instruction to individual learners or groups of learners, including stress-adapted students. For example, designing curricula and instructional practices to ensure that students work together on interdependent tasks benefits college students from working-class but not middle-class backgrounds (Dittmann et al., 2020). Likewise, conducting oral language assessments in a contextually appropriate manner enhances the performance of Black but not White children from low-income families (Fagundes et al., 1998). Finally, self-affirmation interventions that have students describe their families' values or their individual cultural backgrounds typically improve the academic performance of students of color, but not other students (Celeste et al., 2021; Covarrubias et al., 2016).

The *differentiated classroom* (Tomlinson, 2014) provides a strong model for implementing individualized instruction, including the different kinds of teaching and learning strategies discussed herein. Differentiated instruction was originally developed to provide alternatives for gifted students who were not adequately challenged by standard content and to allow inclusion of students with learning disabilities in mainstream classrooms. Differentiated instruction is now commonly used in primary and secondary educational setting (Bernacki et al., 2021) as a way to modify curriculum and instruction to provide alternatives for students who learn in different ways and have different prior knowledge, skills, and interests (Tomlinson, 2014). The idea is to recognize and build on the different capacities that students bring to the classroom by creating a variety of paths toward achieving learning goals within a single classroom (as opposed to segregating students). Systematic reviews indicate that differentiated instruction has small to moderate positive effects on learning outcomes, particularly when implemented well (Deunk et al., 2018; Smale-Jacobse et al., 2019). Differentiated instruction on the basis of specific feedback or progress monitoring is one of the most strongly empirically supported practices for improving educational achievement among socioeconomically disadvantaged students (Dietrichson et al., 2017). In the differentiated classroom, teaching methods used to enhance learning among stress-adapted students can differ from methods used with other students.

At the same time, it is important to note that we are not advocating for differentiated instruction on the basis of learning styles. The learning styles model, which stipulates that learning can be optimized by personalizing instruction to match learners' stated preferences for processing/organizing information in particular ways (e.g., learning by doing vs. reading texts, visual vs. auditory learning), has not been empirically supported (Pashler et al., 2009; Willingham et al., 2015). By contrast, differentiated instruction on the basis of prior knowledge and skills is an evidence-based practice (Bernacki et al., 2021; Deunk et al., 2018). The strategies articulated herein for leveraging hidden talents in education (e.g., modifying instructional practices to directly harness stress-adapted skills, building on hidden talents to extend knowledge) build on prior knowledge and skills. Research is needed to determine the efficacy of implementing these strategies universally versus tailoring them through differentiated instruction.

Finally, experiences of childhood adversity are not uniform. This reality underscores the likely importance of differentiated instruction. Different children face different adaptive problems (e.g., threat versus unpredictability) that may promote the development of different skills (see Section 1.1). It is important, therefore, not to conceptualize stress-adapted students in terms of a unitary skill set. In her work on culturally responsive teaching, Gay (2018) recommends that teachers begin by getting to know their students and the different assets they bring to the classroom. This applies to pedagogy based on hidden talents as well.

5.6 Conclusion

One of the great challenges facing educators is that many, if not most, schoolchildren do not like classroom educational experiences (e.g., Gray, 2013, 2020). This may be especially true of stress-adapted schoolchildren, who often disengage from school and may not find it relevant to what they want (e.g., Richardson et al., 2016; Robles et al., 2019; Sanders et al., 2020). Some stress-adapted students may even experience school as a hostile and alien place (as do a significant number of Black students; Ladson-Billings, 1995). Low motivation and engagement thus stand as serious obstacles in the way of educational programs serving stress-adapted students, especially when there is a mismatch between the lives of students outside of school and what they experience inside of school. This does not mean that stress-adapted students are inherently detached from school; indeed, schools can be structured to get buy-in and cooperation from stress-adapted students (see Wilson et al., 2011). However, as discussed throughout this section, standard school curriculum and instructional practices (including measurement and evaluation) do not adequately align with the skill sets, ways of knowing, goals, values, and motives of stress-adapted students.

The KEEP program, as well as the social dominance, ethnomathematics, food routines, street vending, mathematical thinking, and oral narrative examples reviewed in this section, demonstrate the value of orienting instruction and curriculum around concrete, contextually relevant problems that stress-adapted students are already motivated to solve. Such students tend to be drawn to real-world thinking and problem-solving situations and "have a pragmatic outlook that encourages their preference for concreteness in learning, for practical applications of knowledge in their world, and for examples that both come from and harken back to their world" (VanTassel-Baska, 2018, p. 69). One form of schooling that converges with this practical orientation is career and technical education, where learning of academic concepts (e.g., math, science) is embedded in real-world problems and applications (e.g., automotive technology, health occupations); in other words, career and technical education may provide a good fit (match rather than mismatch) to the preferences and values of many stress-adapted students (Richardson et al., 2016), even if their abilities afford other educational and employment opportunities as well.

Applying these ideas to education, we have proposed three teaching and learning strategies relevant to leveraging hidden talents: (a) modify instructional practices to directly harness stress-adapted skills (e.g., working memory updating, collaborative abilities); (b) anchor curriculum in skills and concepts that are ecologically relevant in harsh environments (e.g., negotiating social dominance hierarchies, price knowledge and recall of daily purchases); and (c) build on hidden talents to extend knowledge (e.g., mathematical skills in street economies, oral narrative fluency). Each of these strategies situate teaching and learning within the lived experiences, skills, and knowledge of stress-adapted students and, therefore, should improve motivation and performance, regardless of subject area, and reduce the mismatch between stress-adapted traits and classroom environments. Such mismatch could be further reduced by employing assessment strategies that focus students on the importance of mastery as opposed to performance and require collaborative work to achieve goals. This latter method is already commonly used in Japanese schools, which often assess achievement based on how well student work groups perform on collective assignments (Cave, 2004; Holloway, 1988).

Given the challenges facing stress-adapted students, the most successful interventions may involve whole-school reforms or bundling of best practices, which often includes tailoring to individual students. Leveraging hidden talents could be one component of a bundle of evidence-based practices. As proof of principle, KEEP exemplifies a successful schoolwide intervention based on leveraging the capacities and cultural capital of a minoritized group experiencing significant socioeconomic adversity and marginalization.

6 Incorporating Hidden Talents into Social Work Theory and Practice

In addition to educational applications, there are translational implications of the hidden talents approach for professions that work with children and families facing adversity (e.g., clinical psychology, counseling, social work). As an example, we focus on the field of social work, which is the largest provider of behavioral and mental health services in the United States, working with children and families across many systems of care (Bureau of Labor Statistics, 2014). Social work has a widely accepted ethos as a strengths-based profession that is geared toward being client-led, emphasizes self-determination, and views clients as resourceful and resilient rather than as a sum of their deficits/challenges (Saleebey, 1996; Zastrow & Hessenauer, 2017). Social work is also guided by a person-in-environment frame that considers all layers of the social environment (i.e., micro, meso, and macro) in addressing social functioning (Garbarino, 2017). At face value, the strengths-based, empowerment, and ecologically centered approach to clients distinguishes social work from other helping or counseling professions (i.e., psychology, counseling) and makes it compatible with the hidden talents model.

Yet despite this professed ethos, the strengths-based approach in social work has been criticized for various shortcomings, both in regard to implementation and as a guiding philosophy. In terms of producing positive and measurable client outcomes, some have argued that "working with strengths" lacks an empirical or measurement basis (Loue, 2018). There is also ambiguity regarding if and how social workers actually employ strengths-based practices in various contexts and practice settings (Gray, 2011). Indeed, the strengths-based perspective often ends up focusing on deficits regardless of the label, value system, or discourse (Gray, 2011). Thus, there remains a chasm between the "theory of strengths-based work" and how it is operationalized in research and practice. Given the current state of the field, strengths-based work may be a guiding "practice" without a clear road map or empirical scaffold (Loue, 2018).

The hidden talents model offers an empirical approach to identifying and measuring stress-adapted skills, and to developing strengths-based interventions that actually harness those skills. This approach is distinct from, yet related to, the traditional social-work diagnostic and treatment model. Social work practice, which is environmentally based and works with clients to adapt their behavior and/or their environment to ameliorate social functioning, involves two primary approaches to intervention with children experiencing behavioral or developmental problems (Garbarino, 2017). The first is try to fix the child's behavioral problems in order to *conform* to the environment (such as the school classroom, the family, or other child settings). The goal of such interventions is to adapt the child's behavior to become less disruptive to the surrounding people and context. In a school classroom, for example, this could involve interventions to enhance student-teacher relationship quality (e.g., Poling et al., 2022) or reduce hostile attribution bias (e.g., Hiemstra et al., 2019). The second approach is to modify the environment, resources, or setting to *mitigate* the problem and promote more harmony between the person and the environment. For example, a social worker might set up a student with learning disabilities in an inclusion classroom that employs differentiated instruction to attend to the student's strengths or needs. This second approach is closer to our current focus on leveraging stress-adapted skills. However, the hidden talents model does not rely on identifying unique (idiosyncratic) weaknesses or strengths of different people; rather, it targets identifying a coherent set of skills that are promoted through exposures to adversity and thus are typically maintained or enhanced in stress-adapted youth, relative to their other skills. The hidden talents approach underscores the distinction between modifying the person or the environment to promote functionality in mainstream settings (as per the social-work diagnostic and treatment model) and capitalizing on unique skills that are enhanced by adversity. Taken together, these approaches are different but complementary.

The hidden talents approach could potentially be applied to many contexts where social intervention occurs with children and youth, such as schools, family work, child welfare, mental health, and other contexts. It also may be particularly applicable to settings that work with adjudicated youth, meaning youth who have contact with the justice system. In both research and practice, the juvenile justice field has a long tradition of assuming that the behavior of youth who come into contact with the law is guided by a host of deficits across multiple domains. These deficits are assumed to be individual (e.g., intellectual, personality), family centered (e.g., poor parenting, lack of structure, maltreatment), and community centered (e.g., gangs, neighborhood adversity, poverty) (Stouthamer-Loeber et al., 2002). By this view, delinquency, or lawbreaking behavior in childhood and adolescence, results from a combination of these factors.

Along these lines, the very popular Risk-Needs-Responsivity (RNR) model (Hoge, 2002) has become the prevailing modality in the United States and other Western nations for assessment and case planning for youth who are adjudicated as delinquent. The RNR model is an evidence-based method of using assessment to classify risk, address deficits, and create targeted plans for intervention. Some assessments stemming from RNR evaluate strengths, but there is a strong focus on the essential question of how to remedy personal deficits in youth so that they can become law-abiding citizens. In this sense, the US juvenile justice field – particularly in practice – is often focused on "fixing" pathology, only identifying strengths as a means to mitigate the pathology. However, an emerging body of work has questioned this approach, including its empirical foundations (Byrne & Lurigio, 2009; Elliott et al., 2020) and the persistent blame on individual youth to the neglect of contextual factors such as racism, poverty, and experiences of adversity (Campbell et al., 2018).

Although youth justice interventions are firmly rooted in deficit perspectives, qualitative and ethnographic research on system-involved youth has identified potential hidden talents that arise from living in harsh, unpredictable environments. The early work of sociologist Elijah Anderson, who coined the term "code of the street" (Anderson, 1999), illustrates the nuances of how those affected by neighborhood disorganization are able to "code switch" for self-protection (meaning they swiftly and effectively adapt to different social settings). Along these lines, Abrams and Terry's (2017) qualitative study *"Everyday Desistance"* identifies how formerly incarcerated youth are able to effectively manage a host of complex daily decisions, reading the environment for safety or danger cues and reacting to them promptly, assessing people quickly for integrity or genuineness, and exercising great resourcefulness in the face of hardships. For example, some of the formerly incarcerated youth in their study were able to navigate mainstream employment opportunities while still appeasing their former gang colleagues and thereby keeping themselves and their families safe from harm. They knew what to wear and how to speak and portray themselves in different circumstances. Although *Everyday Desistance* did not set out to identify hidden talents, it presents an ethnographic view of navigating life following exposures to both harsh community conditions and carceral facilities that may illuminate a diversity of hidden talents that could be applied to leadership, employment, and other life goals. Such hidden talents are not captured in the traditional RNR paradigm or other diagnostic assessments that focus on risk and protective factors.

In sum, the hidden talents approach has the potential to highlight and assess skills that qualitative work has uncovered but not measured. In addition to focusing on traditional risk and protective factors in the lives of adjudicated youth, the hidden talents model raises an alternative set of questions: What do these youth do well (i.e., what skills have they developed to deal with significant challenges within their lived environments)? How can employers develop career opportunities that capitalize on these hidden talents? Addressing these questions could help to locate concrete jobs and skills for youth, identify appropriate educational settings, and transform settings that offer rehabilitation and opportunities for thriving.

6.1 Racial Discrimination, Critical Consciousness, and Development of Hidden Talents

The hidden talents model also has implications for social work practice with youth of color affected by racism or race-related stress. In our earlier discussion of hidden talents as adaptive intelligence (Section 4), we described the niche of childhood adversity. Children and youth growing up in that niche experience threat, deprivation, and/or unpredictability in pervasive and enduring ways. Accordingly, we have conceptualized hidden talents as a form of adaptive intelligence that reflects particular skills related to solving adaptive problems encountered in the niche of childhood adversity. So far, however, our analysis of hidden talents has not considered racism or race-related stress explicitly. This is a limitation because racial discrimination is clearly a form of harshness – it is linked to increased morbidity and mortality (e.g., Barbarin et al., 2020; Beach et al., 2022) – and is distinct from other, more general forms of harshness such as low income and economic marginalization (Beach et al., 2022). Racial discrimination is also a source of environmental unpredictability, as experienced through stochastic events such as random harassment by police (e.g., Hipwell et al., 2018; Testa et al., 2022).

Theory and research is needed to identify specific skills related to solving adaptive problems posed by experiences of racial discrimination (see Barbarin et al., 2020, for an initial discussion). Such knowledge would enable racism-related experiences to be more systematically incorporated into the hidden talents framework. Ideally, theory and research in this domain would be guided by ethnographic knowledge and conducted collaboratively with experts in understanding how children and youth experience and cope with racism. Studies of racial socialization (e.g., how parents of color teach skills to prepare their children to navigate potentially discriminatory situations, such as how to handle themselves when stopped by police; see Anderson & Stevenson, 2019) afford a starting point for this work. We see this as an important future direction for the hidden talents model, as delineating stress-adapted skills that develop in response to racism and race-related stress could inform intervention and practice in constructive ways (e.g., supporting a nonstigmatizing, strength-based approach). Below in this section we consider this issue in relation to critical consciousness.

At the same time, we must not lose sight of the larger goal of eradicating global and national structural racism. Racism needs to be rooted out of the policies, practices, and institutions that perpetuate anti-Blackness, which stems from colonialism and slavery and has been perpetuated in American social policies, laws, and institutions (Kendi, 2019). We recognize that the hidden talents approach assumes some degree of racism and race-related stress in society at present – and thus the need to locate stress-adapted skills shaped by experiences of racial discrimination. We see this is an interim measure, however, which can help all people thrive until the more important goal of realizing an antiracist society is achieved.

The field of social work has a strong emphasis on social justice (Dominelli, 2002), including antioppressive practices that recognize imbalances in power/ access to resources and aim to address those imbalances. This occurs not only through direct service and advocacy on behalf of clients, particularly those facing oppression and marginalization, but also through system change and eradicating root causes of oppression (e.g., Corneau & Stergiopoulos, 2012; Dalrymple & Burke, 1995; Dominelli, 2002). One strategy within the antioppression framework is antiracism, which has been defined as "forms of thought and/or practice that seek to confront, eradicate, and/or ameliorate racism" (Bonnett, 2000, p. 4). In practice, antioppressive and antiracist social work focus on empowerment of service users, including recognizing and building on the life experiences, belief systems, pride, and strengths of minoritized and racialized groups (Corneau & Stergiopoulos, 2012; Svetaz et al., 2020). At a broader level, antioppressive and antiracist strategies for social intervention seek to root out sources of discrimination and oppression through social policy and macro social work (Dominelli, 2002)

Although empowerment and antioppression/antiracism work has not specifically incorporated hidden talents, it has focused on critical consciousness as a form of positive youth development (Barbarin et al., 2020; Sakamoto & Pitner, 2005; Svetaz et al., 2020). *Critical consciousness* can be understood as a set of competencies involved in enacting social change by critically analyzing the inequitable or oppressive social conditions faced by marginalized youth and taking critical action against those conditions (e.g., Hope et al., 2020; Roy et al., 2019).

Individuals facing the adaptive problem of racial discrimination tend to employ a variety of coping strategies, including critical consciousness/action behavior (Hope et al., 2020; Roy et al., 2019). Among Black adolescents and emerging adults, for example, more stressful experiences of racial discrimination are associated with more antiracism activism, such as confronting others who make racist comments, strong support for Black Lives Matter, and participating in protests and demonstrations (Hope et al., 2022). In turn, critical consciousness/action behavior, in and of itself, may promote ecologically relevant skills that support positive youth development. For example, use of active coping and planning strategies for dealing with racial discrimination experienced at school is associated with greater use of strategic approaches to learning (e.g., relating study material to prior knowledge) (Griffin et al., 2022; see Uriostegui et al., 2021, for a review of links between critical consciousness and academic development). More generally, critical consciousness/action behavior involves complex social/cognitive skills (e.g., perspective taking, abstract thinking), strategic thinking (e.g., proactive anticipation, planning and regulating actions to achieve goals), interpersonal skills, and self-management skills involved in coping with race-related stress (Carey et al., 2021; Griffin et al., 2022; Hope et al., 2022; Larson & Angus, 2011). Antioppressive and antiracist social work, with their central focus on social justice and empowerment, could be extended to explicitly leverage these kinds of stress-adapted skills (i.e., skills related to solving adaptive problems posed by experiences of racial discrimination). This hidden talents-based approach – by guiding child and youth service providers to build on the adaptive culture of minoritized groups facing racism and race-related stress – would complement the current focus of social work on identifying and rooting out imbalances in power/access to resources. It would also complement existing interventions that focus on critical consciousness as a means of promoting personal agency, positive identity, and prosocial development, particularly among Black youth (reviewed in Barbarin et al., 2020; Carey et al., 2021).

6.2 Conclusion

The hidden talents approach moves beyond the routinely practiced and accepted risks and strengths perspective to offer alternative but specific and potentially scalable intervention strategies. Such strategies are relevant for young people in juvenile justice and other practice domains of social work, including children and youth experiencing the impact of racism or race-related stress. The hidden talents model focuses on identifying and harnessing skills that develop through experiences of adversity, such as skills needed to navigate neighborhood risks or to analyze and act against racial discrimination (and potentially other forms of discrimination, such as that faced by sexually- and gender-diverse individuals). At the same time, the model clearly shares some concepts and goals with social work and other disciplines of research and practice concerned with positive development among young people who have experienced adversity (Wray-Lake & Abrams, 2020).

7 The Hidden Talents Approach Compared with Traditional Models of Resilience

The hidden talents model converges in a number of ways with more traditional resilience models that have emerged and evolved over the past five decades in developmental and clinical sciences. Yet the hidden talents approach has unique features that distinguish it from other research on resilience, raising new questions and directions for research with translational implications. In this section, we compare and contrast the hidden talents model with more traditional approaches to the science of resilience (see overview in Table 1).

There are significant similarities in the goals, concepts, and assumptions delineated in the hidden talents approach (Ellis et al., 2017; Ellis, Abrams et al., 2022; Frankenhuis & de Weerth, 2013; Frankenhuis, Young, et al.,

Table 1 Key questions guiding traditional resilience models and the hidden talents model

Traditional resilience models	Hidden talents model
• What processes support the adaptive success of individuals and other systems (e.g., family, communities) in the context of serious challenges?	• What attention, learning, memory, problem-solving, and decision-making skills are promoted by exposures to childhood adversity?
• What are the criteria for evaluating adaptive success at different system levels over the life course? How does the resilience of an individual system depend on resilience in other systems?	• Does expression of these skills depend on current conditions or psychological states (e.g., conditions that make salient the reality of daily stressors and uncertainties)?
• Are there common and universal as well as culturally or situationally unique protective attributes and processes?	• How do different forms of childhood adversity relate to the development of specific skills?
• Can resilience capacity be nurtured in development or boosted in the context of current or impending adversity to promote successful adaptation?	• Can stress-adapted skills that enable individuals to function in harsh, unpredictable environments be leveraged to promote success in mainstream contexts, such as schools and work places?

2020) and resilience models articulated by developmental and clinical scientists (Aburn et al., 2016; Cicchetti, 2013; Luthar et al., 2015; Masten et al., 2021; Ungar et al., 2013). Resilience science emerged as researchers studying risk for psychopathology recognized that many people were developing well *despite* exposures to acute and chronic adversity (Luthar et al., 2000; Masten, 2001; Rutter, 1987). The hidden talents model extends this approach by recognizing that many people develop specialized abilities *because of* exposures to adversity. From the outset, the goal motivating resilience research was to uncover processes underlying positive adaptation in contexts of risk, in order to inform efforts to promote the success and health of children, their families, and societies. The hidden talents approach has similar goals: to identify strengths and ultimately promote the success and well-being of stress-adapted individuals in ways that benefit children and youth, their families, and society.

Both models focus on strengths and adaptive capabilities, departing from deficit-based and diathesis-stress models that dominated theory and practice models in psychiatry, psychology, education, and other applied social sciences earlier in the twentieth century. Resilience science has had a transformative influence on intervention research and practice in multiple disciplines concerned with child and family welfare (Masten, 2018). Models broadened to include positive goals, measures of strengths and resources, and strategies for mitigating risk, promoting assets, and mobilizing adaptive processes, in direct counterpoint to deficit models that emphasized risks, vulnerabilities, deficiencies, symptoms, and interventions to address these problems. Both hidden talents and traditional resilience models offer a more positive and hopeful perspective on the challenges encountered by individuals, families, and communities in the face of adversity. Both approaches confront the discouraging and one-sided messages arising from narrow discussions of research on "toxic stress" or "adverse childhood experiences" that focus on risks to health or well-being – messages conveyed to teachers, social workers, and others who work with children experiencing substantial social and economic adversity – and neglect the marked variation in outcomes observed among individuals exposed to such adversities.

Despite these similarities, there also are notable differences between traditional resilience models and the hidden talents model. First and foremost, the two approaches focus on substantively different questions (as presented in Table 1). Further, reflecting their different theoretical origins, the hidden talents model and traditional resilience models differ in their conceptualizations of adaptation. The hidden talents model is rooted in an evolutionary-developmental framework (Section 1.1) and related concepts of adaptive intelligence (Section 4); it emphasizes developmental adaptation to harsh, unpredictable environments, focusing on specific and measurable skills that are shaped by adversity in ways that enable individuals to function adaptively (e.g., survive, control resources) under stressful conditions (Ellis et al., 2017; Frankenhuis & de Weerth, 2013). Although not all stress-adapted skills are socially desirable, a key assumption of the hidden talents approach is that a subset of stress-adapted skills have practical value that can be leveraged for positive ends, even if those skills are not currently being applied to outcomes or goals valued by the dominant culture or society.

In contrast to the focus of the hidden talents model on developmental adaptations to adversity (which encompass negative as well as positive traits), resilience models focus on the subset of individuals who display positive adaptation despite experiencing significant adversity. The criteria for positive adaptation in resilience studies are usually normative (reflecting the values of the dominant culture) with respect to the community or population under study, ranging from mental health to competence in developmental tasks expected for individuals of different ages in the context of a given society, culture, and time in history (Masten, 2018). People who experience significant adversity but do not show positive adaptation by normative standards are not described as manifesting resilience, even though such individuals may display stress-adapted skills. The difference between these approaches is underscored in situations where youth are doing "poorly" (or not participating at all) in mainstream contexts such as school or formal employment (where their behavior is viewed as maladaptive according to dominant cultural values), yet they are functioning well in alternative contexts, such as dangerous neighborhoods, threatening or unstable home environments, precarious social relationships, gangs, the schoolyard, or street economies.

Research on hidden talents highlights positive and potentially unique capabilities of people adapted to harsh, unpredictable environments, in an effort to identify and measure skills honed by their experiences that may be transferable to success in other contexts. This approach both converges with and diverges from approaches within the resilience field that have examined positive changes that can result from exposures to adversity. One area of work has focused on *posttraumatic growth*: "The extent to which survivors of traumatic events perceive personal benefits, including changes in perceptions of self, relationships with others, and philosophy of life, accruing from their attempts to cope with trauma and its aftermath" (Tedeschi & Calhoun, 1996, p. 458). Another line of research has examined *steeling effects* (e.g., Rutter, 2012): The potential for moderate stress exposures to enhance one's capacity to adapt to and cope with subsequent stressors, strengthening resilience-related psychological resources (e.g., self-efficacy, optimism) in a manner analogous to pathogen exposures improving immune function (see Oshri et al., 2022). Both of these positive responses to stress – personal growth and enhanced psychological resources – are conceptually distinct from hidden talents. Specifically, posttraumatic growth and steeling effects diverge from hidden talents in terms of target domain (i.e., criterion-referenced skill levels are not focal variables) and criteria for judging positive adaptation (adhering to normative standards used in resilience models).

In the hidden talents framework, youth who would have been viewed as "maladaptive" in many past studies of resilience (e.g., because of their conduct at school) are studied in relation to cognitive and behavioral adaptations to their lived environments and the skills they develop in that context (i.e., adaptive intelligence). Some of these skills may be shared by adversity-exposed youth who have been studied in resilience models, given that some people who are stress-adapted function well in both normative contexts (e.g., school) and harsh environments (e.g., dangerous neighborhoods). However, the study of stress-adapted youth has the potential to uncover and highlight the competencies of young people often viewed as maladjusted, even by youth themselves, many of whom have been marginalized in society (e.g., due to their struggles in or disengagement from normative contexts). This effort to address a key "white space" in our knowledge about adversity effects on development offers fresh directions for research, with the potential to inform interventions tailored to leverage the skills of stress-adapted people. As a step in this direction, Barbarin et al. (2020) have proposed combining the hidden talents approach with more traditional models of positive youth development and resilience to advance research and interventions for African American boys and young men.

Although resilience-based interventions target change at many points across the lifespan, there has been considerable focus on nurturing the foundational development of resilience in early childhood – during periods of rapid social and neuropsychological development – when change can have cascading effects on future human and social capital (Cicchetti, 2013; Masten & Cicchetti, 2016). Likewise, the hidden talents approach has provided a useful framework for studying adaptations to adversity in young children (e.g., Davies et al., 2022; Li et al., 2021; Rifkin-Graboi et al., 2021); however, hidden talents-based interventions may be especially well suited to people who have come of age in harsh, unpredictable environments and developed stress-adapted skills in that context (see Section 1.2). Importantly, the hidden talents approach does not attempt to change stress-adapted skills (which might be best accomplished early in life); it focuses on *leveraging such skills for positive ends or changing the context to take advantage of these skills.* In the future, interventions could work with the skill sets of stress-adapted young people to afford them expanded opportunities for academic and occupational success, as well as for achieving personal success in contexts that matter to them. Without such interventions, hidden talents may be underutilized at a cost to individuals and society.

8 Conclusion

In this Element, we present a hidden talents approach to understanding human development in the context of adversity, emphasizing the skills that children develop when growing up in harsh, unpredictable environments. Overlooking these skills has been an error of omission in past theory and research – an error that remains pervasive. For example, a recent policy report (*Society for Research in Child Development Statement of the Evidence*) made recommendations for educational policy and practice to support students of color during the COVID-19 pandemic (Yip, 2020). Of the numerous recommendations, 100 percent focused on mitigating risk or ameliorating deficits; none focused on leveraging skills that children and youth with histories of adversity and marginalization bring to the table.

The goal of this Element is to begin filling in this gap. Although the study of hidden talents is an emerging field with various theoretical and methodological challenges (see Frankenhuis, Young et al., 2020), the hidden talents framework extends more traditional approaches to stress and development by identifying, valuing, and seeking to utilize stress-adapted skills. This approach affords a well-rounded view of people who live with adversity that avoids stigma and communicates a novel, distinctive, and strength-based message.

Importantly, this message does not downplay the realities of childhood adversity and its association with individual differences in social/cognitive skills. However, the hidden talents model conceptualizes this association in a novel way. Deficit-based models assume that the link between childhood adversity and variation in social/cognitive skills reflects disparities in mental abilities. By contrast, the hidden talents model assumes that this link results partly – or even largely – from *mismatch* between the social/cognitive skills of stress-adapted people and (a) the kinds of skills that are typically assessed in research and educational settings and (b) the ways/contexts in which those skills are assessed. When this mismatch is reduced, hidden talents can be expected to emerge. In practice, that means hidden talents should be revealed when researchers test for theoretically relevant stress-adapted skills, and when test settings and the content of testing materials are ecologically relevant and concrete. Although these assumptions of the hidden talents model require further testing, each section of this Element presents theory and research consilient with these ideas. Our goal, as an interdisciplinary team of authors, was to build out the hidden talents model from diverse strands of knowledge, ranging from evolutionary-developmental models of adversity to theory and research on neural plasticity, adaptive intelligence, education, social work, and resilience.

Hidden talents, as conceptualized from an evolutionary-developmental perspective, reflect particular skills and forms of knowledge that enable one to function (e.g., survive, obtain resources, navigate significant challenges) within the constraints imposed by harsh, unpredictable environments. Such environments impose developmental tradeoffs, which are apparent in both the potential costs and benefits of developmental adaptations to stress. Tradeoffs are instantiated in patterns of brain development following exposures to early adversity; the juxtaposition of stress-adapted skills (e.g., faster-maturing learning behaviors, better goal-directed behavior in ecologically relevant contexts, stress-adapted decision-making strategies) and other stress-mediated phenotypes (e.g., increased anxiety, reduced cognitive control, truncated developmental plasticity) express such tradeoffs. As represented by the two arrows pointing toward "success in normative environments" in Figure 1, our view is that hidden talents can offset many potential costs of adversity, if environments are structured to actualize stress-adapted skills and leverage them toward positive ends. Traditional approaches to theory and practice in child-serving settings have mostly failed to acknowledge hidden talents – what stress-adapted children and youth *can* do – because of the focus on perceived misbehavior and what they are *not doing*.

Although the current empirical evidence base is modest, with some mixed findings and null results that call for further research, children who grow up in more harsh and unpredictable environments appear to develop enhanced attention and memory for negative emotionally laden or stressful information (e.g., rapid identification of potential danger); greater attunement to other people and social information/relationships (e.g., empathic accuracy, emotion recognition); enhanced reward-oriented problem-solving (e.g., detecting/extracting fleeting or unpredictable rewards from the environment); and heightened abilities for flexibly switching between tasks or mental sets and tracking novel environmental information (e.g., attention shifting, working memory updating). Future research is needed to determine the extent to which the expression of these skills depends on current levels of stress or uncertainty. Further, as shown in a large cultural literature, many instrumental competencies develop in response to environmental demands faced by particular social or cultural groups and play an integral role in adapting to the environment. Such competencies are known as cultural capital. Research in this area may be well-positioned to uncover an array of hidden talents, especially in minoritized and marginalized groups. Some examples discussed in this Element include advanced narrative language skills, navigational abilities, practical knowledge of animals and hunting, ethnobotanical knowledge, collaborative abilities, and critical consciousness. These skill sets may be just the tip of the iceberg. Although diverse data sources support the hidden talents approach, much more research is needed to uncover a high-resolution map of stress-adapted skills.

The hidden talents model has its roots in developmental, cognitive, evolutionary, educational, and cultural psychology as well as neuroscience and animal behavior. That is to say, it is multidisciplinary in nature. Applications of the hidden talents approach are well-positioned to foster interdisciplinary and transdisciplinary collaboration across diverse sectors and disciplines, including psychology, psychiatry, pediatrics, school counseling, social work, marital and family counseling, and other fields concerned with child and family welfare. This approach has implications for instruction, assessment, and intervention, not only for children and youth growing up in harsh environments, but for all young people. Children and youth need to be assessed in ways that capitalize on or take into account their adaptive intelligence – their ability to accomplish tasks that reflect significant challenges within the constraints of their lived environments. Such assessments could help locate concrete jobs and skills for youth, identify appropriate educational and classroom contexts, and transform settings that offer rehabilitation in ways that potentiate the success of stress-adapted people. Teaching and learning strategies could be redesigned to build on the specific talents that students bring to the classroom, such as by anchoring instruction in concrete, contextually relevant problems that stress-adapted children and youth are already motivated to solve. Employing such strategies to promote success in people with adverse life experiences fits into a broad resilience framework, but brings a unique focus on leveraging stress-adapted skills.

In total, the hidden talents approach opens new perspectives for educators, policy makers, families, and youth themselves to reframe the effects of adversity. Societies can scarcely afford to waste the hidden talents of their children and youth; harnessing these strengths could help stress-adapted individuals achieve their full potential and lead more healthy, satisfying, and productive lives.

References

Abrams, L. S., & Terry, D. (2017). *Everyday Desistance: The Transition to Adulthood among Formerly Incarcerated Youth*. New Brunswick: Rutgers University Press. http://doi.org/10.36019/9780813574493

Aburn, G., Gott, M., & Hoare, K. (2016). What is resilience? An integrative review of the empirical literature. *Journal of Advanced Nursing, 72*, 980–1000. http://doi.org/10.1111/jan.12888.

Acosta, J. D., Whitley, M. D., May, L. W. et al. (2016). *Stakeholder Perspectives on a Culture of Health*. Santa Monica, CA: RAND.

Adair, J. K., Colegrove, K. S. S., & McManus, M. E. (2017). How the word gap argument negatively impacts young children of Latinx immigrants' conceptualizations of learning. *Harvard Educational Review, 87*(3), 309–334. http://doi.org/10.17763/1943-5045-87.3.309.

Anderson, E. (1999). *Code of the street: Decency, violence, and the moral life of the inner city*. New York: W. W. Norton.

Anderson, B. A., Laurent, P. A., & Yantis, S. (2011). Value-driven attentional capture. *Proceedings of the National Academy of Sciences, 108*, 10367–10371. http://doi.org/10.1073/pnas.1104047108.

Anderson, R. E., & Stevenson, H. C. (2019). RECASTing racial stress and trauma: Theorizing the healing potential of racial socialization in families. *American Psychologist, 74*(1), 63–75. https://doi.org/10.1037/amp0000392.

Bagot, R. C., van Hasselt, F. N., Champagne, D. L. et al. (2009). Maternal care determines rapid effects of stress mediators on synaptic plasticity in adult rat hippocampal dentate gyrus. *Neurobiology of Learning and Memory, 92*, 292–300. http://doi.org/10.1016/j.nlm.2009.03.004.

Banerjee, A. V., Bhattacharjee, S., Chattopadhyay, R., & Ganimian, A. J. (2017). *The Untapped Math Skills of Working Children in India: Evidence, Possible Explanations, and Implications*. Unpublished Manuscript.

Barbarin, O. A., Tolan, P. H., Gaylord-Harden, N., & Murry, V. (2020). Promoting social justice for African-American boys and young men through research and intervention: A challenge for developmental science. *Applied Developmental Science, 24*(3), 196–207. http://doi.org/10.1080/10888691.2019.1702880.

Baron-Cohen, S., Wheelwright, S., Hill, J., Raste, Y., & Plumb, I. (2001). The "reading the mind in the eyes" Test revised version: A study with normal adults, and adults with Asperger syndrome or high-functioning autism.

The Journal of Child Psychology and Psychiatry and Allied Disciplines, *42*(2), 241–251. http://dx.doi.org/10.1111/1469-7610.00715.

Bath, K. G., Manzano-Nieves, G., & Goodwill, H. (2016). Early life stress accelerates behavioral and neural maturation of hippocampus in male mice. *Hormones and Behavior*, *82*, 64–71. http://doi.org/10.1016/j.yhbeh.2016.04.010.

Beach, S. R., Gibbons, F. X., Carter, S. E. et al. (2022). Childhood adversity predicts black young adults' DNA methylation-based accelerated aging: A dual pathway model. *Development and Psychopathology*, *34*(2), 689–703. http://doi.org/10.1017/S0954579421001541.

Belsky, J. (2019). Early-life adversity accelerates child and adolescent development. *Current Directions in Psychological Science*, *28*, 241–246. http://doi.org/10.1177/0963721419837670.

Belsky, J., Steinberg, L., & Draper, P. (1991). Childhood experience, interpersonal development, and reproductive strategy. *Child Development*, *62*, 647–670. https://doi.org/10.1111/j.1467-8624.1991.tb01558.x.

Bender, K., Thompson, S. J., McManus, H., Lantry, J., & Flynn, P. M. (2007). Capacity for survival: Exploring strengths of homeless street youth. *Child and Youth Care Forum*, *36*, 25–42. http://doi.org/10.1007/s10566-006-9029-4.

Bernier, A., Dégeilh, F., Leblanc, É. et al. (2019). Mother–infant interaction and child brain morphology: A multidimensional approach to maternal sensitivity. *Infancy*, *24*, 120–138. http://doi.org/10.1111/infa.12270.

Bernacki, M. L., Greene, M. J., & Lobczowski, N. G. (2021). A systematic review of research on personalized learning: Personalized by whom, to what, how, and for what purpose (s)? *Educational Psychology Review*, *33*(4), 1675–1715. http://doi.org/10.1007/s10648-021-09615-8.

Bernacki, M. L., & Walkington, C. (2018). The role of situational interest in personalized learning. *Journal of Educational Psychology*, *110*(6), 864–881. http://doi.org/10.1037/edu0000250.

Bjornsdottir, R. T., Alaei, R., & Rule, N. O. (2017). The perceptive proletarian: Subjective social class predicts interpersonal accuracy. *Journal of Nonverbal Behavior*, *41*, 185–201. http://doi.org/10.1007/s10919-016-0248-6.

Blackwell, K. A., Chatham, C. H., Wiseheart, M., & Munakata, Y. (2014). A developmental window into trade-offs in executive function: The case of task switching versus response inhibition in 6-year-olds. *Neuropsychologia*, *62*, 356–364. http://doi.org/10.1016/j.neuropsychologia.2014.04.016.

Blair, C., & Raver, C. C. (2012). Child development in the context of adversity: Experiential canalization of brain and behavior. *American Psychologist*, *67*(4), 309–318. http://doi.org/10.1037/a0027493.

Blair, C., & Raver, C. C. (2014). Closing the achievement gap through modification of neurocognitive and neuroendocrine function: Results from a cluster randomized controlled trial of an innovative approach to the education of children in kindergarten. *PLoS ONE*, *9*, e112393. http://doi.org/10.1371/journal.pone.0112393.

Bogdan, R., Williamson, D. E., & Hariri, A. R. (2012). Mineralocorticoid receptor Iso/Val (rs5522) genotype moderates the association between previous childhood emotional neglect and amygdala reactivity. *American Journal of Psychiatry*, *169*(5), 515–522. http://doi.org/10.1176/appi.ajp.2011.11060855.

Bolund, E. (2020). The challenge of measuring trade-offs in human life history research. *Evolution and Human Behavior*, *41*(6), 502–512. http://doi.org/10.1016/j.evolhumbehav.2020.09.003.

Bonnett, A. (2000). *Anti-racism*. London: Routledge. https://doi.org/10.4324/9780203976098.

Brady, L. M., Germano, A. L., & Fryberg, S. A. (2017). Leveraging cultural differences to promote educational equality. *Current Opinion in Psychology*, *18*, 79–83. http://doi.org/10.1016/j.copsyc.2017.08.003.

Brienza, J. P., & Grossmann, I. (2017). Social class and wise reasoning about interpersonal conflicts across regions, persons and situations. *Proceedings of the Royal Society B*, *284*: 20171870. http://doi.org/10.1098/rspb.2017.1870.

Bureau of Labor Statistics. (2014). *Occupational Outlook Handbook, 2014-15 Edition*. U.S. Bureau of Labor Statistics. www.bls.gov/ooh/community-and-social-service/social-workers.htm#tab-6.

Byrne, J. M., & Lurigio, A. J. (2009). Separating science from nonsense: Evidence-based research, policy, and practice in criminal and juvenile justice settings. *Victims and Offenders*, *4*(4), 303–310. http://doi.org/10.1080/15564880903260512.

Cabeza de Baca, T., Barnett, M. A., & Ellis, B. J. (2016). The development of the child unpredictability schema: Regulation through maternal life history trade-offs. *Evolutionary Behavioral Sciences*, *10*(1), 43–55. https://doi.org/10.1037/ebs0000056.

Calarco, J. M. (2018). *Negotiating Opportunities: How the Middle Class Secures Advantages in School*. New York: Oxford University Press.

Callaghan, B. L., & Richardson, R. (2011). Maternal separation results in early emergence of adult-like fear and extinction learning in infant rats. *Behavioral Neuroscience*, *125*, 20–28. http://doi.org/10.1037/a0022008.

Callaghan, B. L., Sullivan, R. M., Howell, B., & Tottenham, N. (2014). Early adversity and the maturation of emotion circuits–cross-species analysis. *Developmental Psychobiology*, *56*, 1635–1650. https://doi.org/10.1002/dev.21260.

Callaghan, B. L., & Tottenham, N. (2016). The stress acceleration hypothesis: Effects of early-life adversity on emotion circuits and behavior. *Current Opinion in Behavioral Sciences*, *7*, 76–81. http://doi.org/10.1016/j.cobeha .2015.11.018.

Campbell, C., Papp, J., Barnes, A., Onifade, E., & Anderson, V. (2018). Risk assessment and juvenile justice: An interaction between risk, race, and gender. *Criminology & Public Policy*, *17*(3), 525–545. http://doi.org/10.1111/1745-9133.12377.

Carey, R. L., Akiva, T., Abdellatif, H., & Daughtry, K. A. (2021). "And school won't teach me that!" Urban youth activism programs as transformative sites for critical adolescent learning. *Journal of Youth Studies*, *24*(7), 941–960. http://doi.org/10.1080/13676261.2020.1784400.

Carpenter, T. P., Fennema, E., Peterson, P. L., Chiang, C. P., & Loef, M. (1989). Using knowledge of children's mathematics thinking in classroom teaching: An experimental study. *American Educational Research Journal*, *26*, 499–531. http://doi.org/10.3102/00028312026004499.

Carraher, T. N., Carraher, D. W., & Schliemann, A. D. (1985). Mathematics in the streets and in schools. *British Journal of Developmental Psychology*, *3*, 21–29. http://doi.org/10.1111/j.2044-835X.1985.tb00951.x.

Carver, R. P. (1969). Use of a recently developed listening comprehension test to investigate the effect of disadvantagement upon verbal proficiency. *American Educational Research Journal*, *6*(2), 263–270. http://doi.org/ 10.3102/00028312006002263.

Cave, P. (2004). "Bukatsudô": The educational role of Japanese school clubs. *Journal of Japanese Studies*, *30*, 383–415. http://doi.org/10.1353/jjs.2004 .0041.

Ceci, S. J. (1991). How much does schooling influence general intelligence and its cognitive components? A reassessment of the evidence. *Developmental Psychology*, *27*(5), 703–722. http://doi.org/10.1037/0012-1649.27.5.703.

Celeste, L., Baysu, G., Phalet, K., & Brown, R. (2021). Self-affirmation and test performance in ethnically diverse schools: A new dual-identity affirmation intervention. *Journal of Social Issues*, *77*(3), 824–850. http://doi.org/ 10.1111/josi.12418.

Champagne, D. L., Bagot, R. C., van Hasselt, F. et al. (2008). Maternal care and hippocampal plasticity: Evidence for experience-dependent structural plasticity, altered synaptic functioning, and differential responsiveness to glucocorticoids and stress. *Journal of Neuroscience*, *28*, 6037–6045. http://doi.org/ 10.1523/JNEUROSCI.0526-08.2008.

Chisholm, J. S., Quinlivan, J. A., Petersen, R. W., & Coall, D. A. (2005). Early stress predicts age at menarche and first birth, adult attachment, and expected lifespan. *Human Nature, 16*(3), 233–265. http://doi.org/10.1007/s12110-005-1009-0.

Cicchetti, D. (2013). Annual research review: Resilient functioning in maltreated children – past, present, and future perspectives. *Journal of Child Psychology and Psychiatry, 54*, 402–422. http://doi.org/10.1111/j.1469-7610.2012.02608.x.

Clements, D. H., Sarama, J., Spitler, M. E., Lange, A. A., & Wolfe, C. B. (2011). Mathematics learning by young children in an intervention based on learning trajectories: A large-scale cluster randomized trial. *Journal for Research in Mathematics Education, 42*, 127–166. http://doi.org/10.5951/jresematheduc.42.2.0127.

Clinton, V., & Walkington, C. (2019). Interest-enhancing approaches to mathematics curriculum design: Illustrations and personalization. *The Journal of Educational Research, 112*(4), 495–511. http://doi.org/10.1080/00220671.2019.1568958.

Cole, M., & Means, B. (1981). *Comparative Studies of How People Think.* Cambridge, MA: Harvard University Press.

Colich, N. L., Rosen, M. L., Williams, E. S., & McLaughlin, K. A. (2020). Biological aging in childhood and adolescence following experiences of threat and deprivation: A systematic review and meta-analysis. *Psychological Bulletin, 146*(9), 721–764. http://doi.org/10.1037/bul0000270.

Committee on Developments in the Science of Learning. (1999). *How People Learn: A Report of the National Research Council of the National Academy of Science.* Washington, DC: National Academy Press. https://doi.org/10.17226/9853.

Corneau, S., & Stergiopoulos, V. (2012). More than being against it: Anti-racism and anti-oppression in mental health services. *Transcultural Psychiatry, 49*(2), 261–282. http://doi.org/10.1177/1363461512441594.

Covarrubias, R., Herrmann, S. D., & Fryberg, S. A. (2016). Affirming the interdependent self: Implications for Latino student performance. *Basic and Applied Social Psychology, 38*(1), 47–57. https://doi.org/10.1080/01973533.2015.1129609.

Crouzevialle, M., & Darnon, C. (2019). On the academic disadvantage of low social class individuals: Pursuing performance goals fosters the emergence of the achievement gap. *Journal of Educational Psychology, 111*, 1261–1272. http://doi.org/10.1037/edu0000349.

Dahlman, S., Bäckström, P., Bohlin, G., & Frans, Ö. (2013). Cognitive abilities of street children: Low-SES Bolivian boys with and without experience of living in the street. *Child Neuropsychology, 19*, 540–556. http://doi.org/10.1080/09297049.2012.731499.

Dalrymple, J., & Burke, B. (1995). *Anti-oppressive Practice. Social Care and the Law.* Maidenhead: Open University Press.

Daly, M., & Wilson, M. (2005). Carpe diem: Adaptation and devaluing the future. *The Quarterly Review of Biology, 80,* 55–60. http://doi.org/10.1086/431025.

Dang, J., Xiao, S., Zhang, T. et al. (2016). When the poor excel: Poverty facilitates procedural learning. *Scandinavian Journal of Psychology, 57,* 288–291. http://doi.org/10.1111/sjop.12292.

D'angiulli, A., Lipina, S. J., & Olesinska, A. (2012). Explicit and implicit issues in the developmental cognitive neuroscience of social inequality. *Frontiers in Human Neuroscience, 6,* 254. http://doi.org/10.3389/fnhum.2012.00254.

da Silva Ferreira, G. C., Crippa, J. A., & de Lima Osório, F. (2014). Facial emotion processing and recognition among maltreated children: a systematic literature review. *Frontiers in Psychology, 5,* 1460. http://doi.org/10.3389/fpsyg.2014.01460.

Davies, P. T., Thompson, M. J., Li, Z., & Sturge-Apple, M. L. (2022). The cognitive costs and advantages of children's exposure to parental relationship instability: Testing an evolutionary-developmental hypothesis. *Developmental Psychology, 58*(8), 1485–1499. http://doi.org/10.1037/dev0001381.

Davis, H. E. (2014). *Variable Education Exposure and Cognitive Task Performance among the Tsimane Forager-Horticulturalists.* PhD Dissertation, University of New Mexico.

Davis, H. E., & Cashdan, E. (2019). Spatial cognition, navigation, and mobility among children in a forager-horticulturalist population, the Tsimané of Bolivia. *Cognitive Development, 52,* 100800. http://doi.org/10.1016/j.cogdev.2019.100800.

Davis, H. E., Stack, J., & Cashdan, E. (2021). Cultural change reduces gender differences in mobility and spatial ability among seminomadic pastoralist-forager children in northern Namibia. *Human Nature, 32*(1), 178–206. http://doi.org/10.1007/s12110-021-09388-7.

Davis, H. E., Stieglitz, J., Tayo, A. M., Kaplan, H., & Gurven, M. (2021). The formal schooling niche: Longitudinal evidence from Amazonia, Bolivia demonstrates that higher school quality augments differences in children's abstract reasoning. *PsyArXiv.* https://doi.org/10.31234/osf.io/d3sgq.

Deary, I. J., Whalley, L. J., & Starr, J. M. (2009). *A Lifetime of Intelligence: Follow-up Studies of the Scottish Mental Surveys of 1932 and 1947.* American Psychological Association. Washington, DC. http://doi.org/10.1037/11857-000.

Delgado, H., Aldecosea, C., Menéndez, Ñ. et al. (2022). Socioeconomic status differences in children's affective decision-making: The role of awareness in the Children's Gambling Task. *Developmental Psychology, 58*(9), 1716–1729. http://doi.org/10.1037/dev0001382.

Del Giudice, M., & Crespi, B. J. (2018). Basic functional trade-offs in cognition: An integrative framework. *Cognition, 179*, 56–70. http://doi.org/10.1016/j.cognition.2018.06.008.

Del Giudice, M., Ellis, B. J., & Shirtcliff, E. A. (2011). The adaptive calibration model of stress responsivity. *Neuroscience & Biobehavioral Reviews, 35*, 1562–1592. http://doi.org/10.1016/j.neubiorev.2010.11.007.

Del Giudice, M., Gangestad, S. W., & Kaplan, H. S. (2015). Life history theory and evolutionary psychology. In D. M. Buss (Ed.), *The Handbook of Evolutionary Psychology*. Vol.1, foundations (2nd ed., pp. 88–114). New York: John Wiley. http://doi.org/10.1002/9781119125563.evpsych102.

Deming, D. (2009). Early childhood intervention and life-cycle skill development: Evidence from head start. *American Economic Journal: Applied Economics, 1*, 111–134. http://doi.org/10.1257/app.1.3.111.

Deunk, M. I., Smale-Jacobse, A. E., de Boer, H., Doolaard, S., & Bosker, R. J. (2018). Effective differentiation practices: A systematic review and meta-analysis of studies on the cognitive effects of differentiation practices in primary education. *Educational Research Review, 24*, 31–54. http://doi.org/10.1016/j.edurev.2018.02.002.

Deveney, C. M., Chen, S. H., Wilmer, J. B. et al. (2018). How generalizable is the inverse relationship between social class and emotion perception?. *PloS one, 13*(10), e0205949. http://doi.org/10.1371/journal.pone.0205949.

Dickerson, K. L., & Quas, J. A. (2021). Perceived life expectancy, environmental unpredictability, and behavior in high-risk youth. *Journal of Applied Developmental Psychology, 77*, 101344. http://doi.org/10.1016/j.appdev.2021.101344.

Dietrichson, J., Bøg, M., Filges, T., & Klint Jørgensen, A. M. (2017). Academic interventions for elementary and middle school students with low socioeconomic status: A systematic review and meta-analysis. *Review of Educational Research, 87*(2), 243–282. http://doi.org/10.3102/0034654316687036.

Dietze, P., & Knowles, E. D. (2021). Social class predicts emotion perception and perspective-taking performance in adults. *Personality and Social Psychology Bulletin, 47*(1), 42–56. http://doi.org/10.1177/0146167220914116.

Dietze, P., Olderbak, S., Hildebrandt, A., Kaltwasser, L., & Knowles, E. D. (2022). A Lower-Class Advantage in Face Memory. *Personality and Social Psychology Bulletin, 0*(0). https://doi.org/10.1177/01461672221125599.

Distefano, R., Schubert, E. C., Finsaas, M. C. et al. (2020). Ready? Set. Go! A school readiness programme designed to boost executive function skills in preschoolers experiencing homelessness and high mobility.

European Journal of Developmental Psychology, 17(6), 877–894. http:// doi.org/10.1080/17405629.2020.1813103.

Dittmann, A. G., Stephens, N. M., & Townsend, S. S. (2020). Achievement is not class-neutral: Working together benefits people from working-class contexts. *Journal of Personality and Social Psychology. 119*(3), 517–539. http://doi.org/10.1037/pspa0000194

Doebel, S. (2020). Rethinking executive function and its development. *Perspectives on Psychological Science, 15*(4), 942–956. http://doi.org/ 10.1177/1745691620904771.

Doebel, S., & Munakata, Y. (2018). Group influences on engaging self-control: Children delay gratification and value it more when their in-group delays and their out-group doesn't. *Psychological Science, 29*(5), 738–748. http://doi .org/10.1177/0956797617747367.

Dominelli, L. (2002). *Anti Oppressive Social Work Theory and Practice.* New York: Palgrave Macmillan. http://doi.org/10.1007/978-1-4039-1400-2.

Duncan, G. J., Magnuson, K., & Votruba-Drzal, E. (2017). Moving beyond correlations in assessing the consequences of poverty. *Annual Review of Psychology, 68*, 413–434. http://doi.org/10.1146/annurev-psych-010416-044224.

Duquennois, C. (2022). Fictional money, real costs: Impacts of financial salience on disadvantaged students. *American Economic Review, 112*(3), 798–826. http://doi.org/10.1257/aer.20201661.

Durkee, P. K., Lukaszewski, A. W., von Rueden, C. R. et al. (2022). Niche diversity predicts personality structure across 115 nations. *Psychological Science, 33*(2), 285–298. http://doi.org/10.1177/09567976211031571.

Durkin, K., Lipsey, M. W., Farran, D. C., & Wiesen, S. E. (2022). Effects of a statewide pre-kindergarten program on children's achievement and behavior through sixth grade. *Developmental Psychology, 58*(3), 470–484. http:// doi.org/10.1037/dev0001301.

Durlak, J. A., Weissberg, R. P., Dymnicki, A. B., Taylor, R. D., & Schellinger, K. B. (2011). The impact of enhancing students' social and emotional learning: A meta-analysis of school-based universal interventions. *Child Development, 82*, 405–432. http://doi.org/10.1111/j.1467-8624.2010.01564.x.

Dutra, N. B., Chen, L., Anum, A. et al. (2022). Examining relations between performance on non-verbal executive function and verbal self-regulation tasks in demographically-diverse populations. *Developmental Science, 25*(5): e13228. http://doi.org/10.1111/desc.13228.

Eisen, M. L., Goodman, G. S., Qin, J., Davis, S., & Crayton, J. (2007). Maltreated children's memory: accuracy, suggestibility, and psychopathology. *Developmental Psychology, 43*(6), 1275–1294. http://doi.org/10.1037/ 0012-1649.43.6.1275.

Elliott, D. S., Buckley, P. R., Gottfredson, D. C., Hawkins, J. D., & Tolan, P. H. (2020). Evidence-based juvenile justice programs and practices: A critical review. *Criminology & Public Policy, 19*(4), 1305–1328. http://doi.org/10.1111/1745-9133.12520.

Ellis, B. J. (2004). Timing of pubertal maturation in girls: an integrated life history approach. *Psychological Bulletin, 130*(6), 920–958. http://doi.org/10.1037/0033-2909.130.6.920.

Ellis, B. J., Abrams, L. S., Masten, A. S. et al. (2022). Hidden talents in harsh environments. *Development and Psychopathology, 34*(1), 95–113. http://doi.org/10.1017/S0954579420000887.

Ellis, B. J., Bianchi, J., Griskevicius, V., & Frankenhuis, W. E. (2017). Beyond risk and protective factors: An adaptation-based approach to resilience. *Perspectives on Psychological Science, 12*, 561–587. http://doi.org/10.1177/1745691617693054.

Ellis, B. J., & Del Giudice, M. (2014). Beyond allostatic load: Rethinking the role of stress in regulating human development. *Development and Psychopathology, 26*, 1–20. http://doi.org/10.1017/S0954579413000849.

Ellis, B. J., & Del Giudice, M. (2019). Developmental adaptation to stress: An evolutionary perspective. *Annual Review of Psychology, 70*, 111–139. http://doi.org/10.1146/annurev-psych-122216-011732.

Ellis, B. J., Del Giudice, M., Dishion, T. J., Figueredo, A. J., Gray, P., Griskevicius, V., Hawley, P. H., Jacobs, W. J., James, J., Volk, A. A., & Wilson, D. S. (2012). The evolutionary basis of risky adolescent behavior: Implications for science, policy, and practice. *Developmental Psychology, 48*(3), 598–623. https://doi.org/10.1037/a0026220.

Ellis, B. J., Figueredo, A. J., Brumbach, B. H., & Schlomer, G. L. (2009). Fundamental dimensions of environmental risk: Impact of harsh versus unpredictable environments on the evolution and development of life history strategies. *Human Nature, 20*, 204–268. http://doi.org/10.1007/s12110-009-9063-7.

Ellis, B. J., Sheridan, M. A., Belsky, J., & McLaughlin, K. A. (2022). Why and how does early adversity influence development? Toward an integrated model of dimensions of environmental experience. *Development and Psychopathology, 34*(2), 447–471. http://doi.org/10.1017/S0954579421001838.

Ellwood-Lowe, M. E., Whitfield-Gabrieli, S., & Bunge, S. A. (2021). Brain network coupling associated with cognitive performance varies as a function of a child's environment in the ABCD study. *Nature Communications, 12*(1), 1–14. http://doi.org/10.1038/s41467-021-27336-y.

Estelami, H., & Lehmann, D. R. (2001). The impact of research design on consumer price recall accuracy: An integrative review. *Journal of the*

Academy of Marketing Science, 29(1), 36–49. http://doi.org/10.1177/0092070301291003.

Estelami, H., Lehmann, D. R., & Holden, A. C. (2001). Macro-economic determinants of consumer price knowledge: A meta-analysis of four decades of research. *International Journal of Research in Marketing, 18*(4), 341–355. http://doi.org/10.1016/S0167-8116(01)00044-1.

Evans, G. W., Gonnella, C., Marcynyszyn, L. A., Gentile, L., & Salpekar, N. (2005). The role of chaos in poverty and children's socioemotional adjustment. *Psychological Science, 16*(7), 560–565. http://doi.org/10.1111/j.0956-7976.2005.01575.x.

Evans, G. W., Li, D., & Whipple, S. S. (2013). Cumulative risk and child development. *Psychological Bulletin, 139*, 1342–1396. doi:10.1037/a0031808.

Eyck, H. J., Buchanan, K. L., Crino, O. L., & Jessop, T. S. (2019). Effects of developmental stress on animal phenotype and performance: A quantitative review. *Biological Reviews. 94*(3), 1143–1160. http://doi.org/10.1111/brv.12496.

Fagundes, D. D., Haynes, W. O., Haak, N. J., & Moran, M. J. (1998). Task variability effects on the language test performance of southern lower socioeconomic class African American and Caucasian five-year-olds. *Language, Speech, and Hearing Services in Schools, 29*(3), 148–157. http://doi.org/10.1044/0161-1461.2903.148.

Farah, M. J. (2017). The neuroscience of socioeconomic status: Correlates, causes, and consequences. *Neuron, 96*(1), 56–71. http://doi.org/10.1016/j.neuron.2017.08.034.

Felitti, V. J., Anda, R. F., Nordenberg, D. et al. (1998). Relationship of childhood abuse and household dysfunction to many of the leading causes of death in adults: The Adverse Childhood Experiences (ACE) Study. *American Journal of Preventive Medicine, 14*(4), 245–258. https://doi.org/10.1016/S0749-3797(98)00017-8.

Fields, A., Bloom, P. A., VanTieghem, M. et al. (2021). Adaptation in the face of adversity: Decrements and enhancements in children's cognitive control behavior following early caregiving instability. *Developmental Science, 24*(6), e13133. http://doi.org/10.1111/desc.13133.

Fikrat-Wevers, S., van Steensel, R., & Arends, L. (2021). Effects of family literacy programs on the emergent literacy skills of children from low-SES families: A meta-analysis. *Review of Educational Research, 91*(4), 577–613. http://doi.org/10.3102/0034654321998075.

Flynn, J. R. (2016). *Does Your Family Make You Smarter? Nature, Nurture, and Human Autonomy.* Cambridge: Cambridge University Press. https://doi.org/10.1017/CBO9781316576694.

Flynn, J. R., & Sternberg, R. J. (2020). Environmental effects on intelligence. In R. J. Sternberg (Ed.), *Human Intelligence: An Introduction* (pp. 253–278). Cambridge: Cambridge University Press. http://doi.org/10.1017/97811086 10636.

Fox, S. E., Levitt, P., & Nelson, C. A. (2010). How the timing and quality of early experiences influence the development of brain architecture. *Child Development, 81*, 28–40. http://doi.org/10.1111/j.1467-8624.2009 .01380.x.

Frankenhuis, W. E., & Amir, D. (2022). What is the expected human childhood? Insights from evolutionary anthropology. *Development and Psychopathology, 34*(2), 473–497. http://doi.org/10.1017/S0954579421001401.

Frankenhuis, W. E., & Bijlstra, G. (2018). Does exposure to hostile environments predict enhanced emotion detection? *Collabra: Psychology, 4*(1), 18. http://doi.org/10.1525/collabra.127.

Frankenhuis, W. E., de Vries, S. A., Bianchi, J., & Ellis, B. J. (2020). Hidden talents in harsh conditions? A preregistered study of memory and reasoning about social dominance. *Developmental Science, 23*(4), e12835. http://doi .org/10.1111/desc.12835.

Frankenhuis, W. E., & de Weerth, C. (2013). Does early-life exposure to stress shape or impair cognition? *Current Directions in Psychological Science, 22*, 407–412. http://doi.org/10.1177/0963721413484324.

Frankenhuis, W. E., Nettle, D., & McNamara, J. M. (2018). Echoes of early life: Recent insights from mathematical modeling. *Child Development, 89*(5), 1504–1518. http://doi.org/10.1111/cdev.13108.

Frankenhuis, W. E., Panchanathan, K., & Nettle, D. (2016). Cognition in harsh and unpredictable environments. *Current Opinion in Psychology, 7*, 76–80. http://doi.org/10.1016/j.copsyc.2015.08.011.

Frankenhuis, W. E., Young, E. S., & Ellis, B. J. (2020). The hidden talents approach: Theoretical and methodological challenges. *Trends in Cognitive Sciences, 24*(7), 569–581. http://doi.org/10.1016/j.tics.2020.03.007.

Freier, L., Gupta, P., Badre, D., & Amso, D. (2021). The value of proactive goal setting and choice in 3-to 7-year-olds' use of working memory gating strategies in a naturalistic task. *Developmental Science, 24*(1), e13017. http://doi .org/10.1111/desc.13017.

Fry, C. E. (2018). *Executive Functions, Creativity, and Mental Health in Homeless Young People: Implications for Housing Outcome.* Doctoral Dissertation, Cardiff University.

Furuto, L. H. (2014). Pacific ethnomathematics: Pedagogy and practices in mathematics education. *Teaching Mathematics and its Applications, 33*(2), 110–121. http://doi.org/10.1093/teamat/hru009.

Fyfe, E. R., McNeil, N. M., Son, J. Y., & Goldstone, R. L. (2014). Concreteness fading in mathematics and science instruction: A systematic review. *Educational Psychology Review, 26*(1), 9–25. http://doi.org/10.1007/s10648-014-9249-3.

Fyfe, E. R., & Nathan, M. J. (2019). Making "concreteness fading" more concrete as a theory of instruction for promoting transfer. *Educational Review, 71*(4), 403–422. http://doi.org/10.1080/00131911.2018.1424116.

Gallo, L. C., & Matthews, K. A. (2003). Understanding the association between socioeconomic status and physical health: do negative emotions play a role? *Psychological Bulletin, 129*, 10–51. http://doi.org/10.1037/0033-2909.129.1.10.

Gallimore, R., & Goldenberg, C. (2001). Analyzing cultural models and settings to connect minority achievement and school improvement research. *Educational Psychologist, 36*(1), 45–56. http://doi.org/10.1207/S15326985EP3601_5.

Garbarino, J. (2017). *Children and Families in the Social Environment: Modern Applications of Social Work* (2nd ed.). New York: Routledge.

García Coll, C., Crnic, K., Lamberty, G. et al. (1996). An integrative model for the study of developmental competencies in minority children. *Child Development, 67*(5), 1891–1914. http://doi.org/10.2307/1131600.

Gardner-Neblett, N., & Iruka, I. U. (2015). Oral narrative skills: Explaining the language-emergent literacy link by race/ethnicity and SES. *Developmental Psychology, 51*(7), 889–904. http://doi.org/10.1037/a0039274.

Gardner-Neblett, N., Pungello, E. P., & Iruka, I. U. (2012). Oral narrative skills: Implications for the reading development of African American children. *Child Development Perspectives, 6*, 218–224. http://doi.org/10.1111/j.1750-8606.2011.00225.x.

Gay, G. (2018). *Culturally Responsive Teaching: Theory, Research, and Practice* (3rd ed.). New York: Teachers College Press.

Gee, D. G., Gabard-Durnam, L. J., Flannery, J. et al. (2013). Early developmental emergence of human amygdala–prefrontal connectivity after maternal deprivation. *Proceedings of the National Academy of Sciences, 110*, 15638–15643. http://doi.org/10.1073/pnas.1307893110.

Giangrande, E. J., Beam, C. R., Finkel, D., Davis, D. W., & Turkheimer, E. (2022). Genetically informed, multilevel analysis of the Flynn effect across four decades and three WISC versions. *Child Development, 93*(1), e47–e58. http://doi.org/10.1111/cdev.13675.

Gibb, B. E., Schofield, C. A., & Coles, M. E. (2009). Reported history of childhood abuse and young adults' information-processing biases for facial displays of emotion. *Child Maltreatment, 14*, 148–156. http://doi.org/10.1177/1077559508326358.

Gleason, M. M., Fox, N. A., Drury, S. et al. (2011). Validity of evidence-derived criteria for reactive attachment disorder: Indiscriminately social/disinhibited and emotionally withdrawn/inhibited types. *Journal of the American Academy of Child & Adolescent Psychiatry, 50*(3), 216–231. http://doi.org/10.1016/j.jaac.2010.12.012.

Goldenberg, B. M. (2014). White teachers in urban classrooms: Embracing non-white students' cultural capital for better teaching and learning. *Urban Education, 49*(1), 111–144. http://doi.org/10.1177/0042085912472510.

Goodman, G. S., Quas, J. A., & Ogle, C. M. (2010). Child maltreatment and memory. *Annual Review of Psychology, 61*, 325–351. http://doi.org/10.1146/annurev.psych.093008.100403.

Goudeau, S., & Croizet, J. C. (2017). Hidden advantages and disadvantages of social class: How classroom settings reproduce social inequality by staging unfair comparison. *Psychological Science, 28*(2), 162–170. http://doi.org/10.1177/0956797616676600.

González-Arango, F., Corredor, J., López-Ardila, M. A. et al. (2022). The duality of poverty: a replication of Mani et al. (2013) in Colombia. *Theory and Decision, 92*(1), 39–73. http://doi.org/10.1007/s11238-021-09836-x.

Gottfredson, L. S. (1997). Why *g* matters: The complexity of everyday life. *Intelligence, 24*(1), 79–132. https://doi.org/10.1016/S0160-2896(97)90014-3.

Gottfredson, L. S. (2003). Dissecting practical intelligence theory: Its claims and evidence. *Intelligence, 31*(4), 343–397. https://doi.org/10.1016/S0160-2896(02)00085-5.

Gray, M. (2011). Back to basics: A critique of the strengths perspective in social work. *Families in Society, 92*, 5–11. http://doi.org/10.1606/1044-3894.4054.

Gray, P. (2013). *Free to Learn: Why Unleashing the Instinct to Play Will Make Our Children Happier, More Self-reliant, and Better Students for Life.* New York: Basic Books.

Gray, P. (2020). How children coped in the first months of the pandemic lockdown: Free time, play, family togetherness, and helping out at home. *American Journal of Play, 13*(1), 33–52.

Greenberg, M. T., & Abenavoli, R. (2017). Universal interventions: Fully exploring their impacts and potential to produce population-level impacts. *Journal of Research on Educational Effectiveness, 10*, 40–67. http://doi.org/10.1080/19345747.2016.1246632.

Greenfield, P. M. (1997). You can't take it with you: Why ability assessments don't cross cultures. *American Psychologist, 52*(10), 1115–1124. http://doi.org/10.1037/0003-066X.52.10.1115.

Greenfield, P. M. (2020). Historical evolution of intelligence. In R. J. Sternberg (Ed.), *Cambridge Handbook of Intelligence* (2nd ed., pp. 916–939).

New York: Cambridge University Press. http://doi.org/10.1017/978110
8770422.039.

Griffin, C. B., Gray, D., Hope, E., Metzger, I. W., & Henderson, D. X. (2022).
Do coping responses and racial identity promote school adjustment among
black youth? Applying an equity-elaborated social–emotional learning lens.
Urban Education, 57(2), 198–223. http://doi.org/10.1177/0042085920
933346.

Grigorenko, E. L., Geissler, P. W., Prince, R. et al. (2001). Organization of Luo
conceptions of intelligence: A study of implicit theories in a Kenyan village.
International Journal of Behavioral Development, 25, 367–378. http://doi
.org/10.1080/01650250042000348.

Grigorenko, E. L., Meier, E., Lipka, J. et al. (2004). Academic and practical
intelligence: A case study of the Yup'ik in Alaska. *Learning and Individual
Differences, 14*, 183–207. http://doi.org/10.1016/j.lindif.2004.02.002.

Grossmann, I., & Varnum, M. E. (2011). Social class, culture, and cognition.
Social Psychological and Personality Science, 2, 81–89. http://doi.org/
10.1177/1948550610377119,

Gunnar, M. R., & Reid, B. M. (2019). Early deprivation revisited:
Contemporary studies of the impact on young children of institutional care.
Annual Review of Developmental Psychology, 1, 93–118. http://doi.org/
10.1146/annurev-devpsych-121318-085013.

Gurven, M., Fuerstenberg, E., Trumble, B. et al. (2017). Cognitive performance
across the life course of Bolivian forager-farmers with limited schooling.
Developmental Psychology, 53(1), 160–176. http://doi.org/10.1037/
dev0000175.

Gurven, M., Jaeggi, A. V., Von Rueden, C., Hooper, P. L., & Kaplan, H. (2015).
Does market integration buffer risk, erode traditional sharing practices and
increase inequality? A test among Bolivian forager-farmers. *Human Ecology,
43*(4), 515–530. http://doi.org/10.1007/s10745-015-9764-y.

Gurven, M., Kaplan, H., & Gutierrez, M. (2006). How long does it take to
become a proficient hunter? Implications for the evolution of extended
development and long life span. *Journal of Human Evolution, 51*(5),
454–470. http://doi.org/10.1016/j.jhevol.2006.05.003.

Gurven, M., Kaplan, H., & Supa, A. Z. (2007). Mortality experience of Tsimane
Amerindians of Bolivia: regional variation and temporal trends. *American
Journal of Human Biology: The Official Journal of the Human Biology
Association, 19*(3), 376–398. http://doi.org/10.1002/ajhb.20600.

Guyer, A. E., Kaufman, J., Hodgdon, H. B. et al. (2006). Behavioral alterations
in reward system function: The role of childhood maltreatment and
psychopathology. *Journal of the American Academy of Child & Adolescent*

Psychiatry, *45*, 1059–1067. https://doi.org/10.1097/01.chi.0000227 882.50404.11.

Guyon-Harris, K. L., Humphreys, K. L., Miron, D. et al. (2019). Disinhibited social engagement disorder in early childhood predicts reduced competence in early adolescence. *Journal of Abnormal Child Psychology*, *47*(10), 1735–1745. http://doi.org/10.1007/s10802-019-00547-0.

Hanson, J. L., Nacewicz, B. M., Sutterer, M. J. et al. (2015). Behavioral problems after early life stress: Contributions of the hippocampus and amygdala. *Biological Psychiatry*, *77*, 314–323. http://doi.org/10.1016/j .biopsych.2014.04.020.

Hanson, J. L., van den Bos, W., Roeber, B. J. et al. (2017). Early adversity and learning: Implications for typical and atypical behavioral development. *Journal of Child Psychology and Psychiatry*, *58*, 770–778. http://doi.org/ 10.1111/jcpp.12694.

Hart, B., & Risley, T. R. (1995). *Meaningful Differences in the Everyday Experience of Young American Children*. Baltimore, MD: Paul H. Brookes.

Heberle, A. E., & Carter, A. S. (2015). Cognitive aspects of young children's experience of economic disadvantage. *Psychological Bulletin*, *141*, 723–746. http://doi.org/10.1037/bul0000010.

Heckman, J. J., & Kautz, T. (2013). *Fostering and measuring skills: Interventions that improve character and cognition* (National Bureau of Economic Research Working Paper 19656). Retrieved from the National Bureau of Economic Research. www.nber.org/papers/w19656.pdf.

Hein, T. C., & Monk, C. S. (2017). Research Review: Neural response to threat in children, adolescents, and adults after child maltreatment–a quantitative meta-analysis. *Journal of Child Psychology and Psychiatry*, *58*, 222–230. http://doi.org/10.1111/jcpp.12651.

Hernandez, I. A., Silverman, D. M., & Destin, M. (2021). From deficit to benefit: Highlighting lower-SES students' background-specific strengths reinforces their academic persistence. *Journal of Experimental Social Psychology*, *92*, 104080. http://doi.org/10.1016/j.jesp.2020.104080.

Hiemstra, W., De Castro, B. O., & Thomaes, S. (2019). Reducing aggressive children's hostile attributions: A cognitive bias modification procedure. *Cognitive Therapy and Research*, *43*(2), 387–398. https://doi.org/10.1007/ s10608-018-9958-x.

Hill, S. E., Boehm, G. W., & Prokosch, M. L. (2016). Vulnerability to disease as a predictor of faster life history strategies. *Adaptive Human Behavior and Physiology*, *2*, 116–133. http://doi.org/10.1007/s40750-015-0040-6.

Hipwell, A. E., Beeney, J., Ye, F., Gebreselassie, S. H., Stalter, M. R., Ganesh, D., ... & Stepp, S. D. (2018). Police contacts, arrests and decreasing self-control and personal responsibility among female adolescents. *Journal of Child Psychology and Psychiatry, 59*(12), 1252–1260. https://doi.org/10.1111/jcpp.12914.

Hoff, E. (2013). Interpreting the early language trajectories of children from low-SES and language minority homes: Implications for closing achievement gaps. *Developmental Psychology, 49*(1), 4–14. http://doi.org/10.1037/a0027238.

Hoge, R. D. (2002). Standardized instruments for assessing risk and need in youthful offenders. *Criminal Justice and Behavior, 29*, 380–396. http://doi.org/10.1177/0093854802029004003.

Høgheim, S., & Reber, R. (2015). Supporting interest of middle school students in mathematics through context personalization and example choice. *Contemporary Educational Psychology, 42*, 17–25. http://doi.org/10.1016/j.cedpsych.2015.03.006.

Holloway, S. D. (1988). Concepts of ability and effort in Japan and the United States. *Review of Educational Research, 58*, 327–345. http://doi.org/10.3102/00346543058003327.

Honeycutt, J. A., Demaestri, C., Peterzell, S. et al. (2020). Altered corticolimbic connectivity reveals sex-specific adolescent outcomes in a rat model of early life adversity. *eLife, 9*, e52651. http://doi.org/10.7554/eLife.52651.

Hope, E. C., Smith, C. D., Cryer-Coupet, Q. R., & Briggs, A. S. (2020). Relations between racial stress and critical consciousness for black adolescents. *Journal of Applied Developmental Psychology, 70*, 101184. http://doi.org/10.1016/j.appdev.2020.101184.

Hope, E. C., Volpe, V. V., Briggs, A. S., & Benson, G. P. (2022). Anti-racism activism among Black adolescents and emerging adults: Understanding the roles of racism and anticipatory racism-related stress. *Child Development, 93*(3), 717–731. http://doi.org/10.1111/cdev.13744.

Hostinar, C. E., & Miller, G. E. (2019). Protective factors for youth confronting economic hardship: Current challenges and future avenues in resilience research. *American Psychologist, 74*, 641–652. http://doi.org/10.1037/amp0000520.

Humphreys, K. L., Lee, S. S., Telzer, E. H. et al. (2015). Exploration-exploitation strategy is dependent on early experience. *Developmental Psychobiology, 57*, 313–321. http://doi.org/10.1002/dev.21293.

Jenness, J. L., Peverill, M., Miller, A. B. et al. (2021). Alterations in neural circuits underlying emotion regulation following child maltreatment: A mechanism underlying trauma-related psychopathology. *Psychological Medicine, 51*(11), 1880–1889. http://doi.org/10.1017/S0033291720000641,

Johnson, M. H., Jones, E. J., & Gliga, T. (2015). Brain adaptation and alternative developmental trajectories. *Development and Psychopathology, 27*(2), 425–442. http://doi.org/10.1017/S0954579415000073.

Jones, J. H. (2009). The force of selection on the human life cycle. *Evolution and Human Behavior, 30*(5), 305–314. http://doi.org/10.1016/j.evolhumbehav.2009.01.005.

Jordan, C. (1984). Cultural compatibility and the education of Hawaiian children: Implications for mainland educators. *Educational Research Quarterly, 8*(4), 59–71.

Jordan, C. (1985). Translating culture: From ethnographic information to educational program. *Anthropology & Education Quarterly, 16*(2), 105–123. http://doi.org/10.1525/aeq.1985.16.2.04x0631g.

Jordan, C., Tharp, R. G., & Baird-Vogt, L. (1992). "Just open the door": Cultural compatibility and classroom rapport. In M. Saravia-Shore & S. F. Arvizu (Eds.), *Cross-cultural Literacy: Ethnographies of Communication in Multiethnic Classrooms* (pp. 3–18). New York: Garland. http://doi.org/10.4324/9781351237109-2.

Jury, M., Smeding, A., & Darnon, C. (2015). First-generation students' underperformance at university: The impact of the function of selection. *Frontiers in Psychology, 6*, 710. https://doi.org/10.3389/fpsyg.2015.00710.

Kaplan, H. S., & Lancaster, J. B. (2003). An evolutionary and ecological analysis of human fertility, mating patterns, and parental investment. In K.W. Wachter & R. A. Bulatao (Eds.), *Offspring: Human Fertility Behavior in Biodemographic Perspective* (pp. 170–223).Washington, DC: National Academies Press.

Kendi, I. X. (2019). *How to be an Antiracist*. New York: One world.

Kidd, C., Palmeri, H., & Aslin, R. N. (2013). Rational snacking: Young children's decision-making on the marshmallow task is moderated by beliefs about environmental reliability. *Cognition, 126*, 109–114. http://doi.org/10.1016/j.cognition.2012.08.004.

Kisker, E. E., Lipka, J., Adams, B. L. et al. (2012). The potential of a culturally based supplemental mathematics curriculum to improve the mathematics performance of Alaska Native and other students. *Journal for Research in Mathematics Education, 43*, 75–113. http://doi.org/10.5951/jresematheduc.43.1.0075.

Kitano, M. K. (2010). The role of culture in shaping expectations for gifted students. In J. L. Van Tassel-Baska (Ed.), *Patterns and Profiles of Promising Learners from Poverty* (pp. 11–32). Waco, TX: Prufrock Press.

Kolb, B., & Gibb, R. (2014). Searching for principles of brain plasticity and behavior. *Cortex, 58*(2), 251–260. http://doi.org/10.1016/j.cortex.2013.11.012.

Kopetz, C., Woerner, J. I., MacPherson, L. et al. (2019). Early psychosocial deprivation and adolescent risk-taking: The role of motivation and executive control. *Journal of Experimental Psychology: General, 148*, 388–399. http://doi.org/10.1037/xge0000486.

Kraus, M. W., Côté, S., & Keltner, D. (2010). Social class, contextualism, and empathic accuracy. *Psychological Science, 21*(11), 1716–1723. http://doi.org/10.1177/0956797610387613.

Kraus, M. W., Horberg, E. J., Goetz, J. L., & Keltner, D. (2011). Social class rank, threat vigilance, and hostile reactivity. *Personality and Social Psychology Bulletin, 37*(10), 1376–1388. http://doi.org/10.1177/01461672 11410987.

Kraus, M. W., & Keltner, D. (2009). Signs of socioeconomic status: A thin-slicing approach. *Psychological science, 20*(1), 99–106. http://doi.org/10.1111/j.1467-9280.2008.02251.x.

Kraus, M. W., Piff, P. K., & Keltner, D. (2009). Social class, sense of control, and social explanation. *Journal of Personality and Social Psychology, 97*, 992–1004. http://doi.org/10.1037/a0016357.

Kraus, M. W., Piff, P. K., Mendoza-Denton, R., Rheinschmidt, M. L., & Keltner, D. (2012). Social class, solipsism, and contextualism: How the rich are different from the poor. *Psychological Review, 119*, 546–572. http://doi.org/10.1037/a0028756.

Labov, W. (1970). The logic of nonstandard English. In F. Williams (Ed.), *Language and poverty: Perspectives on a Theme* (pp. 153–189). Markham. http://doi.org/10.1016/B978-0-12-754850-0.50014-3.

Ladson-Billings, G. (1995). But that's just good teaching! The case for culturally relevant pedagogy. *Theory into Practice, 34*(3), 159–165. http://doi.org/10.1080/00405849509543675.

Larson, R. W., & Angus, R. M. (2011). Adolescents' development of skills for agency in youth programs: Learning to think strategically. *Child Development, 82*(1), 277–294. http://doi.org/10.1111/j.1467-8624.2010.01555.x.

Lawler, J. M., Hostinar, C. E., Mliner, S. B., & Gunnar, M. R. (2014). Disinhibited social engagement in postinstitutionalized children: differentiating normal from atypical behavior. *Developmental Psychopathology, 26*, 451–464. http://doi.org/10.1017/S0954579414000054.

Learning Policy Institute & Turnaround for Children. (2021). *Design Principles for Schools: Putting the Science of Learning and Development into Action.* Creative Commons.

Lee, A., Poh, J. S., Wen, D. J. et al. (2019). Maternal care in infancy and the course of limbic development. *Developmental Cognitive Neuroscience, 40*, 100714. http://doi.org/10.1016/j.dcn.2019.100714.

Lee, C. D. (1995a). Signifying as a scaffold for literary interpretation. *Journal of Black Psychology, 21*(4), 357–381. http://doi.org/10.1177/009579849 50214005.

Lee, C. D. (1995b). A culturally based cognitive apprenticeship: Teaching African American high school students skills in literary interpretation. *Reading Research Quarterly, 30*(4), 608–630. http://doi.org/10.2307/ 748192.

Leonard, J. A., Mackey, A. P., Finn, A. S., & Gabrieli, J. D. (2015). Differential effects of socioeconomic status on working and procedural memory systems. *Frontiers in Human Neuroscience, 9,* Article 554. http://doi.org/10.3389/ fnhum.2015.00554.

Leonard, J. A., Romeo, R. R., Park, A. T. et al. (2019). Associations between cortical thickness and reasoning differ by socioeconomic status in development. *Developmental Cognitive Neuroscience, 36,* 100641. http:// doi.org/10.1016/j.dcn.2019.100641.

Levy-Gigi, E., Richter-Levin, G., Okon-Singer, H., Kéri, S., & Bonanno, G. A. (2016). The hidden price and possible benefit of repeated traumatic exposure. *Stress, 19,* 1–7. http://doi.org/10.3109/10253890.2015.1113523.

Leyva, D., Shapiro, A., Yeomans-Maldonado, G., Weiland, C., & Leech, K. (2022). Positive impacts of a strengths-based family program on Latino kindergarteners' narrative language abilities. *Developmental Psychology, 58*(5), 835–847. http://doi.org/10.1037/dev0001332.

Leyva, D., Weiland, C., Shapiro, A., Yeomans-Maldonado, G., & Febles, A. (2022). A strengths-based, culturally responsive family intervention improves Latino kindergarteners' vocabulary and approaches to learning. *Child Development, 93*(2), 451–467. http://doi.org/10.1111/cdev.13698.

Li, Z., Sturge-Apple, M. L., & Davies, P. T. (2021). Contextual risks, child problem-solving profiles, and socioemotional functioning: Testing the specialization hypothesis. *Development and Psychopathology,* 1–13. http://doi .org/10.1017/S0954579421001322.

Lloyd, A., McKay, R. T., & Furl, N. (2022). Individuals with adverse childhood experiences explore less and underweight reward feedback. *Proceedings of the National Academy of Sciences, 119*(4), e2109373119. http://doi.org/ 10.1073/pnas.2109373119.

Loman, M. M., Johnson, A. E., Quevedo, K., Lafavor, T. L., & Gunnar, M. R. (2014). Risk-taking and sensation-seeking propensity in postinstitutionalized early adolescents. *Journal of Child Psychology and Psychiatry, 55,* 1145–1152. http://doi.org/10.1111/jcpp.12208.

Loue, S. (2018). Strengths-based social work: Issues, controversies, and ethical considerations. In A. Sandu & A. Frunza (Eds.), *Ethical issues in social work practice* (pp. 62–81). IGI Global. http://doi.org/10.4018/978-1-5225-3090-9 .ch006.

Love, L., Minnis, H., & O'Connor, S. (2015). Factors associated with indiscriminate friendliness in high-risk children. *Infant Mental Health Journal, 36,* 427–445. http://doi.org/10.1002/imhj.21520.

Lupien, S. J., Ouellet-Morin, I., Hupbach, A., Tu, M. T., Buss, C., Walker, D., . . . McEwen, B. S. (2006). Beyond the stress concept: Allostatic load. A developmental biological and cognitive perspective. In D. Cicchetti, & D. J. Cohen (Eds.), *Developmental Psychopathology*: Vol. 2. *Developmental Neuroscience* (2nd Edition., pp. 578–628). Hoboken, NJ: Wiley.

Luria, A. R. (1976). *Cognitive Development: Its Cultural and Social Foundations.* Cambridge, MA: Harvard University Press.

Luthar, S., Cicchetti, D., & Becker, B. (2000). The construct of resilience: A critical evaluation and guidelines for future work. *Child Development, 71,* 543–562. http://doi.org/10.1111/1467-8624.00164.

Luthar, S. S., Crossman, E. J., & Small, P. J. (2015). Resilience and adversity. In R. M. Lerner (Editor-in-Chief) and M. E. Lamb (Volume Ed.). *Handbook of Child Psychology and Developmental Science. Vol. 3. Socioemotional Processes* (7th ed., pp. 247–286). New York: Wiley. http://doi.org/10.1002/ 9781118963418.childpsy307.

Malindi, M. J., & Theron, L. C. (2010). The hidden resilience of street youth. *South African Journal of Psychology, 40,* 318–326. http://doi.org/10.1177/ 0081246310040003 10.

Mani, A., Mullainathan, S., Shafir, E., & Zhao, J. (2013). Poverty impedes cognitive function. *Science, 341,* 976–980. http://doi.org/10.1126/ science.1238041.

Mareckova, K., Marecek, R., Andryskova, L., Brazdil, M., & Nikolova, Y. S. (2020). Maternal depressive symptoms during pregnancy and brain age in young adult offspring: Findings from a prenatal birth cohort. *Cerebral Cortex, bhaa014. 30*(7), 3991–3999. http://doi.org/10.1093/cercor/bhaa014.

Masten, A. S. (2001). Ordinary magic: Resilience processes in development. *American Psychologist, 56,* 227–238. http://doi.org/10.1037/0003-066X.56.3.227

Masten, A. S. (2018). Resilience theory and research on children and families: Past, present, and promise. *Journal of Family Theory and Review, 10,* 12–31. http://doi.org/10.1111/jftr.12255.

Masten, A. S., & Cicchetti, D. (2016). Resilience in development: Progress and transformation. In D. Cicchetti (Ed.), *Developmental psychopathology, Vol. 4: Risk, Resilience, and Intervention* (3rd ed.) (pp. 271–333). New York: Wiley. http://doi.org/10.1002/9781119125556.devpsy406.

Masten, A. S., Lucke, C. M., Nelson, K. M., & Stallworthy, I. C. (2021). Resilience in development and psychopathology. *Annual Review of Clinical Psychology, 17*, 521–549. https://doi.org/10.1146/annurev-clinpsy-081219-120307.

McCoy, D. C., Raver, C. C., & Sharkey, P. (2015). Children's cognitive performance and selective attention following recent community violence. *Journal of Health and Social Behavior, 56*, 19–36. http://doi.org/10.1177/0022146514567576.

McCrory, E. J., & Viding, E. (2015). The theory of latent vulnerability: Reconceptualizing the link between childhood maltreatment and psychiatric disorder. *Development and Psychopathology, 27*, 493–505. http://doi.org/10.1017/S0954579415000115.

McDermott, C. L., Seidlitz, J., Nadig, A. et al. (2019). Longitudinally mapping childhood socioeconomic status associations with cortical and subcortical morphology. *Journal of Neuroscience, 39*(8), 1365–1373. http://doi.org/10.1523/JNEUROSCI.1808-18.2018.

McEwen, B. S. (2009). The brain is the central organ of stress and adaptation. *Neuroimage, 47*, 911–913. http://doi.org/10.1016/j.neuroimage.2009.05.071.

McEwen, B. S., & Stellar, E. (1993). Stress and the individual: Mechanisms leading to disease. *Archives of Internal Medicine, 153*, 2093–2101. http://doi.org/10.1001/archinte.1993.00410180039004.

McLaughlin, K. A., & Lambert, H. K. (2017). Child trauma exposure and psychopathology: Mechanisms of risk and resilience. *Current Opinion in Psychology, 14*, 29–34. http://doi.org/10.1016/j.copsyc.2016.10.004.

McLaughlin, K. A., Sheridan, M. A., & Lambert, H. K. (2014). Childhood adversity and neural development: deprivation and threat as distinct dimensions of early experience. *Neuroscience & Biobehavioral Reviews, 47*, 578–591. http://doi.org/10.1016/j.neubiorev.2014.10.012.

McLaughlin, K. A., Weissman, D., & Bitrán, D. (2019). Childhood Adversity and Neural Development: A Systematic Review. *Annual Review of Developmental Psychology, 1*, 277–312. http://doi.org/10.1146/annurev-devpsych-121318-084950.

McCrae, R. R., & Costa, P. T., Jr. (1997). Personality trait structure as a human universal. *American Psychologist, 52*(5), 509–516. http://doi.org/10.1037/0003-066X.52.5.509.

Mell, H., Safra, L., Algan, Y., Baumard, N., & Chevallier, C. (2018). Childhood environmental harshness predicts coordinated health and reproductive strategies. *Evolution and Human Behavior, 39*, 1–8. https://doi.org/10.1016/j.evolhumbehav.2017.08.006.

Merrick, M. T., Ford, D. C., Ports, K. A., & Guinn, A. S. (2018). Prevalence of adverse childhood experiences from the 2011-2014 Behavioral Risk Factor Surveillance System in 23 states. *JAMA Pediatrics, 172*, 1038–1044. http://doi.org/10.1001/jamapediatrics.2018.2537.

Michaelson, L. E., & Munakata, Y. (2016). Trust matters: Seeing how an adult treats another person influences preschoolers' willingness to delay gratification. *Developmental Science, 19*, 1011–1019. http://doi.org/10.1111/desc.12388.

Miller, P. J., & Sperry, D. E. (2012). Déjà vu: The continuing misrecognition of low-income children's verbal abilities. In S. T. Fiske & H. R. Markus (Eds.), *Facing Social Class: How Societal Rank Influences Interaction* (pp. 109–130). Thousand Oaks, CA: Russell Sage.

Miller-Cotto, D., Smith, L. V., Wang, A. H., & Ribner, A. D. (2022). Changing the conversation: A culturally responsive perspective on executive functions, minoritized children and their families. *Infant and Child Development, 31*(1), e2286. http://doi.org/10.1002/icd.2286.

Mittal, C., Griskevicius, V., Simpson, J. A., Sung, S., & Young, E. S. (2015). Cognitive adaptations to stressful environments: When childhood adversity enhances adult executive function. *Journal of Personality and Social Psychology, 109*, 604–621. http://doi.org/10.1037/pspi0000028.

Moffett, L., Flannagan, C., & Shah, P. (2020). The influence of environmental reliability in the marshmallow task: An extension study. *Journal of Experimental Child Psychology, 194*, 104821. http://doi.org/10.1016/j.jecp.2020.104821.

Moll, L. C., Amanti, C., Neff, D., & Gonzalez, N. (1992). Funds of knowledge for teaching: Using a qualitative approach to connect homes and classrooms. *Theory into Practice, 31*(2), 132-141. http://doi.org/10.1080/00405849209543534.

Monroe, S. M., & Simons, A. D. (1991). Diathesis-stress theories in the context of life stress research: Implications for the depressive disorders. *Psychological Bulletin,110*, 406–425. http://doi.org/10.1037/0033-2909.110.3.406.

Monroy, M., Cowen, A. S., & Keltner, D. (2022). Intersectionality in emotion signaling and recognition: The influence of gender, ethnicity, and social class. *Emotion.* 22(8), 1980–1988.https://doi.org/10.1037/emo0001082.

Moriceau, S., Shionoya, K., Jakubs, K., & Sullivan, R. M. (2009). Early-life stress disrupts attachment learning: the role of amygdala corticosterone, locus ceruleus corticotropin releasing hormone, and olfactory bulb norepinephrine. *Journal of Neuroscience, 29*, 15745–15755. http://doi.org/10.1523/JNEUROSCI.4106-09.2009.

Nettle, D., Frankenhuis, W. E., & Rickard, I. J. (2013). The evolution of predictive adaptive responses in human life history. *Proceedings of the Royal Society B, 280*, 20131343. http://doi.org/10.1098/rspb.2013.1343.

Nketia, J., Amso, D., & Brito, N. H. (2021). Towards a more inclusive and equitable developmental cognitive neuroscience. *Developmental Cognitive Neuroscience, 52*, 101014. http://doi.org/10.1016/j.dcn.2021.101014.

Noble, K. G., Hart, E. R., & Sperber, J. F. (2021). Socioeconomic disparities and neuroplasticity: Moving toward adaptation, intersectionality, and inclusion. *American Psychologist, 76*(9), 1486–1495. http://doi.org/10.1037/amp 0000934.

Nweze, T., Nwoke, M. B., Nwufo, J. I., Aniekwu, R. I., & Lange, F. (2021). Working for the future: parentally deprived Nigerian Children have enhanced working memory ability. *Journal of Child Psychology and Psychiatry, 62*(3), 280–288. http://doi.org/10.1111/jcpp.13241.

Obradović, J., Sulik, M. J., Finch, J. E., & Tirado-Strayer, N. (2018). Assessing students' executive functions in the classroom: Validating a scalable group-based procedure. *Journal of Applied Developmental Psychology, 55*, 4–13. http://doi.org/10.1016/j.appdev.2017.03.003.

Obradović, J., Yousafzai, A. K., Finch, J. E., & Rasheed, M. A. (2016). Maternal scaffolding and home stimulation: Key mediators of early intervention effects on children's cognitive development. *Developmental Psychology, 52*(9), 1409–1421. http://doi.org/10.1037/dev0000182.

Olsavsky, A. K., Telzer, E. H., Shapiro, M. et al. (2013). Indiscriminate amygdala response to mothers and strangers after early maternal deprivation. *Biological Psychiatry, 74*, 853–860. http://doi.org/10.1016/j.biopsych.2013.05.025.

Ogbu, J. U. (1981). Origins of human competence: A cultural-ecological perspective. *Child Development, 52*, 413–429. http://doi.org/10.2307/1129158.

Ono, M., Kikusui, T., Sasaki, N. et al. (2008). Early weaning induces anxiety and precocious myelination in the anterior part of the basolateral amygdala of male Balb/c mice. *Neuroscience, 156*, 1103–1110. http://doi.org/10.1016/j .neuroscience.2008.07.078.

Orr, D. B., & Graham, W. R. (1968). Development of a listening comprehension test to identify educational potential among disadvantaged junior high school students. *American Educational Research Journal, 5*(2), 167–180. http://doi .org/10.3102/00028312005002167.

Oshri, A., Cui, Z., Carvalho, C., & Liu, S. (2022). Is perceived stress linked to enhanced cognitive functioning and reduced risk for psychopathology? Testing the hormesis hypothesis. *Psychiatry Research, 314*, 114644. http:// doi.org/10.1016/j.psychres.2022.114644.

Panter-Brick, C. (2002). Street children, human-rights and public health: A critique and future directions. *Annual Review of Anthropology, 31,* 147–171. http://doi.org/10.1146/annurev.anthro.31.040402.085359.

Pashler, H., McDaniel, M., Rohrer, D., & Bjork, R. (2008). Learning styles: Concepts and evidence. *Psychological Science in the Public Interest, 9*(3), 105–119. http://doi.org/10.1111/j.1539-6053.2009.01038.x.

Pellegrini, M., Lake, C., Neitzel, A., & Slavin, R. E. (2021). Effective programs in elementary mathematics: A meta-analysis. *AERA Open, 7*(1), 1–29. https://doi.org/10.1177/2332858420986211.

Pepper, G. V., & Nettle, D. (2017). The behavioural constellation of deprivation: Causes and consequences. *Behavioral and Brain Sciences, 40,* e314. http://doi.org/10.1017/S0140525X1600234X.

Perez-Brena, N. J., Rivas-Drake, D., Toomey, R. B., & Umaña-Taylor, A. J. (2018). Contributions of the integrative model for the study of developmental competencies in minority children: What have we learned about adaptive culture? *American Psychologist, 73*(6), 713–726. http://doi.org/10.1037/amp0000292.

Piff, P. K., Kraus, M. W., & Keltner, D. (2018). Unpacking the inequality paradox: The psychological roots of inequality and social class. In J. Olson (Ed.), *Advances in Experimental Social Psychology* (Vol. 57, pp. 53–124). Cambridge, MA: Academic Press.

Pinheiro P. S. (2006). *World Report on Violence against Children.* Geneva, Switzerland: United Nations Secretary-General's Study on Violence Against Children.

Pion, G. M., & Lipsey, M. W. (2021). Impact of the Tennessee Voluntary Prekindergarten Program on children's literacy, language, and mathematics skills: Results from a regression-discontinuity design. *AERA Open, 7*(1), 1–23. http://doi.org/10.1177/23328584211041353.

Pitula, C. E., Wenner, J. A., Gunnar, M. R., & Thomas, K. M. (2017). To trust or not to trust: Social decision-making in post-institutionalized, internationally adopted youth. *Developmental Science, 20,* e12375. http://doi.org/10.1111/desc.12375.

Poling, D., Van Loan, C. L., Garwood, J. D., Zhang, S., & Riddle, D.(2022). Enhancing teacher-student relationship quality: A narrative review of school-based interventions. *Educational Research Review, 37,* 100459. https://doi.org/10.1016/j.edurev.2022.100459.

Pollak, S. D. (2008). Mechanisms linking early experience and the emergence of emotions: Illustrations from the study of maltreated children. *Current Directions in Psychological Science, 17,* 370–375. http://doi.org/10.1111/j.1467-8721.2008.00608.x.

Pollak, S. D., Cicchetti, D., Hornung, K., & Reed, A. (2000). Recognizing emotion in faces: Developmental effects of child abuse and neglect. *Developmental Psychology, 36,* 679–688. http://doi.org/10.1037/0012-1649.36.5.679.

Pollak, S. D., Messner, M., Kistler, D. J., & Cohn, J. F. (2009). Development of perceptual expertise in emotion recognition. *Cognition, 110,* 242–247. http://doi.org/10.1016/j.cognition.2008.10.010.

Pope, S. M., Fagot, J., Meguerditchian, A., Washburn, D. A., & Hopkins, W. D. (2019). Enhanced cognitive flexibility in the seminomadic Himba. *Journal of Cross-Cultural Psychology, 50,* 47–62. http://doi.org/10.1177/0022022118806581.

Posner, J., Cha, J., Roy, A. K. et al. (2016). Alterations in amygdala–prefrontal circuits in infants exposed to prenatal maternal depression. *Translational Psychiatry, 6,* e935. http://doi.org/10.1038/tp.2016.146.

Priniski, S. J., Hecht, C. A., & Harackiewicz, J. M. (2018). Making learning personally meaningful: A new framework for relevance research. *The Journal of Experimental Education, 86*(1), 11–29. http://doi.org/10.1080/00220973.2017.1380589.

Puetz, V. B., Viding, E., Gerin, M. I. et al. (2020). Investigating patterns of neural response associated with childhood abuse v. childhood neglect. *Psychological Medicine, 50*(8), 1398–1407. http://doi.org/10.1017/S003329171900134X.

Qiu, A., Rifkin-Graboi, A., Chen, H. et al. (2013). Maternal anxiety and infants' hippocampal development: Timing matters. *Translational Psychiatry, 3,* e306. http://doi.org/10.1038/tp.2013.79.

Quinlan, R. J. (2007). Human parental effort and environmental risk. *Proceedings of the Royal Society B: Biological Sciences, 274*(1606), 121–125. http://doi.org/10.1098/rspb.2006.3690.

Rapp, C. A., Pettus, C. A., & Goscha, R. J. (2006). Principles of strengths-based policy. *Journal of Policy Practice, 5*(4), 3–18. http://doi.org/10.1300/J508v05n04_02.

Reyes-García, V., Kightley, E., Ruiz-Mallén, I. et al. (2010). Schooling and local environmental knowledge: Do they complement or substitute each other? *International Journal of Educational Development, 30*(3), 305–313. http://doi.org/10.1016/j.ijedudev.2009.11.007.

Reynolds, A. J., Ou, S. R., Mondi, C. F., & Giovanelli, A. (2019). Reducing poverty and inequality through preschool-to-third-grade prevention services. *American Psychologist, 74,* 653–672. http://doi.org/10.1037/amp0000537.

Richardson, G. B., Castellano, M. E., Stone, J. R., & Sanning, B. K. (2016). Ecological and evolutionary principles for secondary education: Analyzing career and tech ed. *Evolutionary Psychological Science, 2*(1), 58–69. http:// doi.org/10.1007/s40806-015-0034-4.

Richardson, K. (2002). What IQ tests test. *Theory & Psychology, 12*(3), 283–314. http://doi.org/10.1177/0959354302012003012.

Richters, J. E., & Cicchetti, D. (1993). Mark Twain meets DSM-III-R: Conduct disorder, development, and the concept of harmful dysfunction. *Development and Psychopathology, 5*, 5–29. https://doi.org/10.1017/S0954579400004235.

Rieder, C., & Cicchetti, D. (1989). Organizational perspective on cognitive control functioning and cognitive-affective balance in maltreated children. *Developmental Psychology, 25*, 382–393. http://doi.org/10.1037/0012-1649.25.3.382.

Rifkin-Graboi, A., Goh, S. K. Y., Chong, H. J. et al. (2021). Caregiving adversity during infancy and preschool cognitive function: adaptations to context?. *Journal of Developmental Origins of Health and Disease, 12*(6), 890–901. http://doi.org/10.1017/S2040174420001348.

Rifkin-Graboi, A., Kong, L., Sim, L. W. et al. (2015). Maternal sensitivity, infant limbic structure volume and functional connectivity: a preliminary study. *Translational Psychiatry, 5*, e668. http://doi.org/10.1038/tp.2015.133.

Rifkin-Graboi, A., Quan, J., Richmond, J. et al. (2018). Greater caregiving risk, better infant memory performance? *Hippocampus, 28*, 497–511. http://doi .org/10.1002/hipo.22949.

Ritchie, S. J., & Tucker-Drob, E. M. (2018). How much does education improve intelligence? A meta-analysis. *Psychological Science, 29*, 1358–1369. http:// doi.org/10.1177/0956797618774253.

Robles, A., Gjelsvik, A., Hirway, P., Vivier, P. M., & High, P. (2019). Adverse childhood experiences and protective factors with school engagement. *Pediatrics, 144*(2), e20182945. http://doi.org/10.1542/peds.2018-2945.

Rogoff, B., Coppens, A. D., Alcalá, L. et al. (2017). Noticing learners' strengths through cultural research. *Perspectives on Psychological Science, 12*, 876–888. http://doi.org/10.1177/1745691617718355.

Rohrbeck, C. A., Ginsburg-Block, M. D., Fantuzzo, J. W., & Miller, T. R. (2003). Peer-assisted learning interventions with elementary school students: A meta-analytic review. *Journal of Educational Psychology, 94*(20), 240–257. http://doi.org/10.1037/0022-0663.95.2.240.

Romeo, R. R., Leonard, J. A., Grotzinger, H. M. et al. (2021). Neuroplasticity associated with changes in conversational turn-taking following a family-based intervention. *Developmental Cognitive Neuroscience, 49*, 100967. http://doi.org/10.1016/j.dcn.2021.100967.

Ross, L. T., & Hill, E. M. (2002). Childhood unpredictability, schemas for unpredictability, and risk taking. *Social Behavior and Personality: An*

International Journal, *30*(5), 453–473. https://doi.org/10.2224/sbp.2002.30.5.453.

Roy, A. L., Raver, C. C., Masucci, M. D., & DeJoseph, M. (2019). "If they focus on giving us a chance in life we can actually do something in this world": Poverty, inequality, and youths' critical consciousness. *Developmental Psychology*, *55*(3), 550–561. http://doi.org/10.1037/dev0000586.

Rutter, M. (1987). Psychosocial resilience and protective mechanisms. *American Journal of Orthopsychiatry*, *57*, 316–331. http://doi.org/10.1111/j.1939-0025.1987.tb03541.x.

Rutter, M. (2012). Resilience as a dynamic concept. *Development and Psychopathology*, *24*, 335–344. http://doi.org/10.1017/S0954579412000028.

Saarinen, A., Keltikangas-Järvinen, L., Jääskeläinen, E. et al. (2021). Early adversity and emotion processing from faces: a meta-analysis on behavioral and neurophysiological responses. *Biological Psychiatry: Cognitive Neuroscience and Neuroimaging*, *6*(7), 692–705. http://doi.org/10.1016/j.bpsc.2021.01.002.

Sackett, P. R., Shewach, O. R., & Dahlke, J. A. (2020). The predictive value of general intelligence. In R. J. Sternberg (Ed.), *Human Intelligence: An Introduction* (pp. 381–414). Cambridge: Cambridge University Press. http://doi.org/10.1017/9781108610636.

Saleebey, D. (1996). The strengths perspective in social work practice: Extensions and cautions. *Social Work*, *41*, 296–305. https://doi.org/10.1093/sw/41.3.296.

Sakamoto, I., & Pitner, R. O. (2005). Use of critical consciousness in anti-oppressive social work practice: Disentangling power dynamics at personal and structural levels. *The British Journal of Social Work*, *35*(4), 435–452. http://doi.org/10.1093/bjsw/bch190.

Sanders, M. T., Welsh, J. A., Bierman, K. L., & Heinrichs, B. S. (2020). Promoting resilience: A preschool intervention enhances the adolescent adjustment of children exposed to early adversity. *School Psychology*, *35*(5), 285–298. http://doi.org/10.1037/spq0000406.

Schmalor, A., & Heine, S. J. (2022). Subjective economic inequality decreases emotional intelligence, especially for people of high social class. *Social Psychological and Personality Science*, *13*(2), 608–617. http://doi.org/10.1177/19485506211024024.

Schwabe, L., & Wolf, O. T. (2013). Stress and multiple memory systems: From "thinking" to "doing." *Trends in Cognitive Sciences*, *17*, 60–68. http://doi.org/10.1016/j.tics.2012.12.001.

Silverman, D. M., Hernandez, I. A., & Destin, M. (2022). Educators' Beliefs About Students' Socioeconomic Backgrounds as a Pathway for Supporting Motivation. *Personality and Social Psychology Bulletin*, *0*(0). https://doi.org/10.1177/01461672211061945.

Silvers, J. A., Goff, B., Gabard-Durnam, L. J. et al. (2017). Vigilance, the amygdala, and anxiety in youths with a history of institutional care. *Biological Psychiatry: Cognitive Neuroscience and Neuroimaging, 2*, 493–501. http://doi.org/10.1016/j.bpsc.2017.03.016.

Singh, R., Gupta, V., & Mondal, A. (2012). Jugaad – From "Making Do" and "Quick Fix" to an innovative, sustainable and low-cost survival strategy at the bottom of the pyramid. *International Journal of Rural Management, 8*(1–2), 87–105. https://doi.org/10.1177/0973005212461995.

Slavin, R. E., Lake, C., Davis, S., & Madden, N. A. (2011). Effective programs for struggling readers: A best-evidence synthesis. *Educational Research Review, 6*(1), 1–26. http://doi.org/10.1016/j.edurev.2010.07.002.

Smaldino, P. E., Lukaszewski, A., von Rueden, C., & Gurven, M. (2019). Niche diversity can explain cross-cultural differences in personality structure. *Nature Human Behaviour, 3*(12), 1276–1283. http://doi.org/10.1038/s41562-019-0730-3.

Smale-Jacobse, A. E., Meijer, A., Helms-Lorenz, M., & Maulana, R. (2019). Differentiated instruction in secondary education: A systematic review of research evidence. *Frontiers in Psychology, 10*, 2366. http://doi.org/10.3389/fpsyg.2019.02366.

Smeding, A., Darnon, C., Souchal, C., Toczek-Capelle, M. C., & Butera, F. (2013). Reducing the socio-economic status achievement gap at university by promoting mastery-oriented assessment. *PLoS ONE, 8*, e71678. http://doi.org/10.1371/journal.pone.0071678.

Snyder, K. E., Fong, C. J., Painter, J. K. et al. (2019). Interventions for academically underachieving students: A systematic review and meta-analysis. *Educational Research Review, 28*, 100294. http://doi.org/10.1016/j.edurev.2019.100294.

Stellar, J. E., Manzo, V. M., Kraus, M. W., & Keltner, D. (2012). Class and compassion: Socioeconomic factors predict responses to suffering. *Emotion, 12*(3), 449–459. http://doi.org/10.1037/a0026508.

Stephens, N. M., Townsend, S. S., & Dittmann, A. G. (2019). Social-class disparities in higher education and professional workplaces: The role of cultural mismatch. *Current Directions in Psychological Science, 28*(1), 67–73. http://doi.org/10.1177/0963721418806506.

Sternberg, R. J. (1999). Successful intelligence: Finding a balance. *Trends in Cognitive Sciences, 3*(11), 436–442. http://doi.org/10.1016/S1364-6613(99)01391-1.

Sternberg, R. J. (2017). Creativity, intelligence, and culture. In V. P. Glaveanu (Ed.), *Palgrave Handbook of Creativity and Culture Research* (pp. 77–99). London: Palgrave. http://doi.org/10.1057/978-1-137-46344-9_5.

Sternberg, R. J. (2019). A theory of adaptive intelligence and its relation to general intelligence. *Journal of Intelligence, 7*, 23. http://doi.org/10.3390/ jintelligence7040023.

Sternberg, R. J. (2021a). *Adaptive Intelligence: Surviving and Thriving in Times of Uncertainty.* New York: Cambridge University Press. http://doi.org/ 10.1017/9781316650554.

Sternberg, R. J. (2021b). Adaptive intelligence: Intelligence is not a personal trait but rather a person x task x situation interaction. *Journal of Intelligence, 9*(4), 58. https://doi.org/10.3390/jintelligence9040058.

Sternberg, R. J., & Hedlund, J. (2002). Practical intelligence, *g*, and work psychology. *Human Performance, 15*(1–2), 143–160. http://doi.org/ 10.1080/08959285.2002.9668088.

Sternberg, R. J., Lipka, J., Newman, T., Wildfeuer, S., & Grigorenko, E. L. (2006). Triarchically-based instruction and assessment of sixth-grade mathematics in a Yup'ik cultural setting in Alaska. *Gifted and Talented International, 21*(2), 6–19. http://doi.org/10.1080/15332276.2006.11673471.

Sternberg, R. J., Nokes, K., Geissler, P. W. et al. (2001). The relationship between academic and practical intelligence: A case study in Kenya. *Intelligence, 29*, 401–418. http://doi.org/10.1016/S0160-2896(01)00065-4.

Steudte-Schmiedgen, S., Stalder, T., Kirschbaum, C. et al. (2014). Trauma exposure is associated with increased context-dependent adjustments of cognitive control in patients with posttraumatic stress disorder and healthy controls. *Cognitive, Affective, & Behavioral Neuroscience, 14*, 1310–1319. http://doi.org/10.3758/s13415-014-0299-2.

Stockard, J., Wood, T. W., Coughlin, C., & Rasplica Khoury, C. (2018). The effectiveness of direct instruction curricula: A meta-analysis of a half century of research. *Review of Educational Research, 88*(4), 479–507. http://doi.org/ 10.3102/0034654317751919.

Stouthamer-Loeber, M., Loeber, R., Wei, E., Farrington, D. P., & Wikström, P.-O. H. (2002). Risk and promotive effects in the explanation of persistent serious delinquency in boys. *Journal of Consulting and Clinical Psychology, 70*(1), 111–123. http://doi.org/10.1037/0022-006X.70.1.111.

Sturge-Apple, M. L., Davies, P. T., Cicchetti, D., Hentges, R. F., & Coe, J. L. (2017). Family instability and children's effortful control in the context of poverty: Sometimes a bird in the hand is worth two in the bush. *Developmental Psychopathology, 29*, 685–696. http://doi.org/10.1017/ S0954579416000407.

Suor, J. H., Sturge-Apple, M. L., Davies, P. T., & Cicchetti, D. (2017). A life history approach to delineating how harsh environments and hawk tempera-ment traits differentially shape children's problem-solving skills. *Journal*

Child Psychology and Psychiatry, *58*, 902–909. http://doi.org/10.1111/jcpp.12718.

Svetaz, M. V., Barral, R., Kelley, M. A. et al. (2020). Inaction is not an option: Using antiracism approaches to address health inequities and racism and respond to current challenges affecting youth. *Journal of Adolescent Health*, *67*(3), 323–325. http://doi.org/10.1016/j.jadohealth.2020.06.017

Szepsenwol, O. (2022). Identifying developmental adaptations to early-life stress. *Infant and Child Development*, *31*(1), e2290. http://doi.org/10.1002/icd.2290.

Tedeschi, R. G., & Calhoun, L. G. (1996). The posttraumatic growth inventory: Measuring the positive legacy of trauma. *Journal of Traumatic Stress*, *9*, 455–471. http://doi.org/10.1002/jts.2490090305.

Teicher, M. H., Samson, J. A., Anderson, C. M., & Ohashi, K. (2016). The effects of childhood maltreatment on brain structure, function and connectivity. *Nature Reviews Neuroscience*, *17*, 652–666. http://doi.org/10.1038/nrn.2016.111.

Testa, A., Turney, K., Jackson, D. B., & Jaynes, C. M. (2022). Police contact and future orientation from adolescence to young adulthood: Findings from the Pathways to Desistance Study. *Criminology*, *60*(2), 263–290. https://doi.org/10.1111/1745-9125.12297.

Tharp, R. G., Jordan, C., Speidel, G. E. et al. (2007). Education and native Hawaiian children: Revisiting KEEP. *Hūlili: Multidisciplinary Research on Hawaiian Well-Being*, *4*(1), 269–317.

Thijssen, S., Collins, P. F., & Luciana, M. (2020). Pubertal development mediates the association between family environment and brain structure and function in childhood. *Development and Psychopathology*, *32*(2), 687–702. http://doi.org/10.1017/S0954579419000580.

Thijssen, S., Muetzel, R. L., Bakermans-Kranenburg, M. J. et al. (2017). Insensitive parenting may accelerate the development of the amygdalamedial prefrontal cortex circuit. *Development and Psychopathology*, *29*, 505–518. https://doi.org/10.1017/S0954579417000141.

Tomlinson, C. A. (2014). *The Differentiated Classroom: Responding to the Needs of All Learners*. Alexandria, VA: Association for Supervision & Curriculum Development.

Tooley, U. A., Bassett, D. S., & Mackey, A. P. (2021). Environmental influences on the pace of brain development. *Nature Reviews Neuroscience*, *22*(6), 372–384. http://doi.org/10.1038/s41583-021-00457-5.

Tottenham, N. (2020). Early adversity and the neotenous human brain. *Biological Psychiatry*, *87*(4), 350–358. http://doi.org/10.1016/j.biopsych.2019.06.018.

Tottenham, N., Hare, T. A., Quinn, B. T. et al. (2010). Prolonged institutional rearing is associated with atypically large amygdala volume and difficulties in emotion regulation. *Developmental Science, 13*, 46–61. http://doi.org/10.1111/j.1467-7687.2009.00852.x.

Ungar, M., Ghazinour, M., & Richter, J. (2013). Annual research review: What is resilience within the social ecology of human development? *Journal of Child Psychology and Psychiatry, 54*, 348–366. http://doi.org/10.1111/jcpp.12025.

Uriostegui, M., Roy, A. L., & Li-Grining, C. P. (2021). What drives you? Black and Latinx youth's critical consciousness, motivations, and academic and career activities. *Journal of Youth and Adolescence, 50*(1), 58–74. http://doi.org/10.1007/s10964-020-01343-6.

Ursache, A., & Noble, K. G. (2016). Neurocognitive development in socioeconomic context: Multiple mechanisms and implications for measuring socioeconomic status. *Psychophysiology, 53*, 71–82. https://doi.org/10.1111/psyp.12547.

VanTassel-Baska, J. (2018). Achievement unlocked: Effective curriculum interventions with low-income students. *Gifted Child Quarterly, 62*, 68–82. http://doi.org/10.1177/0016986217738565.

VanTieghem, M., Korom, M., Flannery, J. et al. (2021). Longitudinal changes in amygdala, hippocampus and cortisol development following early caregiving adversity. *Developmental Cognitive Neuroscience, 48*, 100916. http://doi.org/10.1016/j.dcn.2021.100916.

Vashro, L., & Cashdan, E. (2015). Spatial cognition, mobility, and reproductive success in northwestern Namibia. *Evolution and Human Behavior, 36*(2), 123–129. http://doi.org/10.1016/j.evolhumbehav.2014.09.009.

Villaseñor, A., & Kepner, H. S. (1993). Arithmetic from a problem-solving perspective: An urban implementation. *Journal for Research in Mathematics Education, 24*, 62–69. https://doi.org/10.5951/jresematheduc.24.1.0062.

Vogel, S., Fernández, G., Joëls, M., & Schwabe, L. (2016). Cognitive adaptation under stress: A case for the mineralocorticoid receptor. *Trends in Cognitive Sciences, 20*, 192–203. http://doi.org/10.1016/j.tics.2015.12.003.

Volk, T., & Atkinson, J. (2008). Is child death the crucible of human evolution? *Journal of Social, Evolutionary, and Cultural Psychology, 2*(4), 247–260. http://doi.org/10.1037/h0099341.

Volk, A. A., & Atkinson, J. A. (2013). Infant and child death in the human environment of evolutionary adaptation. *Evolution and Human Behavior, 34*, 182–192. http://doi.org/10.1016/j.evolhumbehav.2012.11.007.

von Stumm, S., & Plomin, R. (2015). Socioeconomic status and the growth of intelligence from infancy through adolescents. *Intelligence, 48*, 30–36. https://doi.org/10.1016/j.intell.2014.10.002.

Vogt, L. A., Jordan, C., & Tharp, R. G. (1987). Explaining school failure, producing school success: Two cases. *Anthropology & Education Quarterly, 18*(4), 276–286. http://doi.org/10.1525/aeq.1987.18.4.04x0019s.

Wakefield, K. L., & Inman, J. J. (1993). Who are the price vigilantes? An investigation of differentiating characteristics influencing price information processing. *Journal of Retailing, 69*(2), 216–233. https://doi.org/10.1016/0022-4359(93)90004-3.

Walkington, C. A. (2013). Using adaptive learning technologies to personalize instruction to student interests: The impact of relevant contexts on performance and learning outcomes. *Journal of Educational Psychology, 105*(4), 932–945. http://doi.org/10.1037/a0031882.

Watson, T., & McLanahan, S. (2011). Marriage meets the Joneses: Relative income, identity, and marital status. *Journal of Human Resources, 46*, 482–517. http://doi.org/10.3368/jhr.46.3.482.

Weisner, T. S., Gallimore, R., & Jordan, C. (1988). Unpackaging cultural effects on classroom learning: Native Hawaiian peer assistance and child-generated activity. *Anthropology & Education Quarterly, 19*(4), 327–353. http://doi.org/10.1525/aeq.1988.19.4.05x0915e.

Weller, J. A., Leve, L. D., Kim, H. K., Bhimji, J., & Fisher, P. A. (2015). Plasticity of risky decision making among maltreated adolescents: Evidence from a randomized controlled trial. *Development and Psychopathology, 27*, 535–551. http://doi.org/10.1017/S0954579415000140.

Willingham, D. T., Hughes, E. M., & Dobolyi, D. G. (2015). The scientific status of learning styles theories. *Teaching of Psychology, 42*(3), 266–271. http://doi.org/10.1177/0098628315589505.

Wilson, D. S., Kauffman Jr, R. A., & Purdy, M. S. (2011). A program for at-risk high school students informed by evolutionary science. *PLoS One, 6*(11), e27826. http://doi.org/10.1371/journal.pone.0027826.

World Bank (2018). *Poverty and Shared Prosperity 2018: Piecing Together the Poverty Puzzle*. Washington, DC: World Bank.

Wray-Lake, L., & Abrams, L. S. (2020). Pathways to civic engagement among urban youth of color. *Monographs of the Society for Research in Child Development, 85*(2), 7–154. http://doi.org/10.1111/mono.12415.

Yeager, D. S., Dahl, R. E., & Dweck, C. S. (2018). Why interventions to influence adolescent behavior often fail but could succeed. *Perspectives on Psychological Science, 13*, 101–122. http://doi.org/10.1177/1745691617722620.

Yip, T. (Ed.) (2020). Addressing inequities in education during the COVID-19 pandemic: How education policy and schools can support historically and currently marginalized children and youth. *Society for Research in Child Development Statement of the Evidence*. Washington, DC: Society for Research in Child Development.

Yosso, T. J. (2005). Whose culture has capital? A critical race theory discussion of community cultural wealth. *Race Ethnicity and Education, 8*(1), 69–91. http://doi.org/10.1080/1361332052000341006.

Young, E. S., Frankenhuis, W. E., DelPriore, D. J., & Ellis, B. J. (2022). Hidden talents in context: Cognitive performance with abstract versus ecological stimuli among adversity-exposed youth. *Child Development, 93*(5), 1493–1510. https://doi.org/10.1111/cdev.13766.

Young, E. S., Frankenhuis, W. E., & Ellis, B. J. (2020). Theory and measurement of environmental unpredictability. *Evolution and Human Behavior, 41*(6), 550–556. http://doi.org/10.1016/j.evolhumbehav.2020.08.006.

Young, E. S., Griskevicius, V., Simpson, J. A., Waters, T. E., & Mittal, C. (2018). Can an unpredictable childhood environment enhance working memory? Testing the sensitized-specialization hypothesis. *Journal of Personality and Social Psychology, 114*, 891–908. http://doi.org/10.1037/pspi0000124.

Yousafzai, A. K., Obradovic, J., Rasheed, M. A. et al. (2016). Effects of responsive stimulation and nutrition interventions on children's development and growth at age 4 years in a disadvantaged population in Pakistan: A longitudinal follow-up of a cluster-randomised factorial effectiveness trial. *The Lancet Global Health, 4*, e548–e558. https://doi.org/10.1016/S2214-109X(16)30100-0.

Zastrow, C., & Hessenauer, S. L. (2017). *Empowerment series: Introduction to social work and social welfare: Empowering people* (12th Edition). Boston, MA: Cengage Learning.

Zelazo, P. D. (2020). Executive function and psychopathology: A neuro developmental perspective. *Annual Review of Clinical Psychology, 16*(1), 431–454. http://doi.org/10.1146/annurev-clinpsy-072319-024242.

Acknowledgments

This Element is adapted with permission from Ellis, Abrams et al. (2022). Development of this Element was supported by the Robert Wood Johnson Foundation (73657) Research Network on Adaptations to Childhood Stress (Directors: Ellis & Frankenhuis). We thank Andrea Dittmann, Diana Leyva, Candace Walkington, and Alex Weiss for their insightful comments on earlier drafts of this Element.

Cambridge Elements ⹀

Applied Evolutionary Science

David F. Bjorklund
Florida Atlantic University

David F. Bjorklund is a Professor of Psychology at Florida Atlantic University in Boca Raton, Florida. He is the Editor-in-Chief of the *Journal of Experimental Child Psychology*, the Vice President of the Evolution Institute, and has written numerous articles and books on evolutionary developmental psychology, with a particular interest in the role of immaturity in evolution and development.

About the Series
This series presents original, concise, and authoritative reviews of key topics in applied evolutionary science. Highlighting how an evolutionary approach can be applied to real-world social issues, many Elements in this series will include findings from programs that have produced positive educational, social, economic, or behavioral benefits. Cambridge Elements in Applied Evolutionary Science is published in association with the Evolution Institute.

Cambridge Elements ≡

Applied Evolutionary Science

Elements in the Series

Printed in the United States
by Baker & Taylor Publisher Services